W. W. Rowe

Patterns
in Russian Literature II:
Notes on Classics

Ardis, Ann Arbor

Ardis Publishers
2901 Heatherway
Ann Arbor, Michigan 48104

Library of Congress Cataloging in Publication Data

Rowe, William Woodin.
Patterns in Russian literature II.

1. Russian literature—19th century—History and
criticism. I. Title.
PG3011.R59   1988   891.7′09′033   88-3440
ISBN 0-87501-054-7 (alk. paper)

Hum
PG
3011
R59
1988

For Eleanor

Contents

Preface

In ancient China, an ailing lady would expose only her hand and wrist from behind a curtain. Yet doctors diagnosed and prescribed with no little success. The microcosm reflected the macrocosm. In the case of a great writer, the written world is unique; its details, characteristic and revealing.

> The writer's art is his real passport. His identity should be immediately recognized by a special pattern or unique coloration. —Vladimir Nabokov

> Like an ice-skater cutting an intricate figure, a major writer may often be tracing patterns, seemingly random or eccentric, around a single, unwavering pivot. His divagations are in fact a constant return. —George Steiner

This book took much longer to develop than my *Nabokov & Others: Patterns in Russian Literature*. The expanded focus adds two writers (Turgenev and Chekhov) to the previous six. There is more emphasis on effects that are obscured or erased in standard English translations. Chapter Fourteen appeared in *Slavic Review*, Vol. 30, No. 1 (March 1971); Chapter Fifteen, in *Slavic and East European Journal*, Vol. 18, No. 4 (Winter 1974)—each in a somewhat different form.

In literary criticism, it is often the daring that stimulates. Obviously, it is dangerous as well. But if readers find parts of this book stimulating and useful, I shall be rewarded. My wife Eleanor aided me greatly. Sydney Schultze and Charles Moser both made numerous valuable suggestions. Of course, I alone am responsible for any errors of fact or interpretation. Unless specified otherwise, translations from the Russian are my own. References (in parentheses) will be to the following editions:

A. P. Chekhov, *Polnoe sobranie sochinenii i pisem v tridtsati tomakh* (Moscow, 1974–83).

L. N. Tolstoi, *Sobranie sochinenii v dvadtsati dvukh tomakh* (Moscow, 1978–85).

F. M. Dostoevskii, *Sobranie sochinenii v desyati tomakh* (Moscow, 1956–58).

I. S. Turgenev, *Sobranie sochinenii v desyati tomakh* (Moscow, 1961–62).

N. V. Gogol', *Polnoe sobranie sochinenij* (Moscow, 1937–52).

M. Yu. Lermontov, *Sobranie sochinenii v chetyryokh tomakh* (Moscow, 1957–58).

A. S. Pushkin, *Polnoe sobranie sochinenii v desyati tomakh* (Moscow, 1962–66).

1

Chekhov: The Birds of Passion

Birds abound in Anton Chekhov's creative works.[1] Remarkably often, people are likened to birds: perhaps no other image is so pervasively revealing of his art. With compassion and detachment, he saw his characters in all their weaknesses, yet with the potential for rising above them. Images of birds—frail and vulnerable, yet capable of glorious flight—aptly suggest the human condition in Chekhov's written world. Most often, he associated bird images with the amorous involvements of his characters. We shall examine these "passion-related" birds and attempt to draw some conclusions about their artistic function.

At the end of "The Lady with the Little Dog" (1899), Anna Sergeevna and Gurov cannot understand ". . . why he was married, and she was married; they were like two migratory birds, a male and a female, caught and forced to live in separate cages." (10:143) This description combines two Chekhovian "birds of passion" motifs. As we shall see, Chekhov sometimes associated bird migration with adultery or leaving a mate. Birds in cages typically suggest difficult or uncomfortable relationships between men and women. Here, the image of caged birds was anticipated by Gurov's "clipped, wingless life" with his own wife, likened to confinement in an insane asylum or prison camp (137).

In *Drama At The Hunt* (1884), Zinoviev's story begins with the words "The husband killed his wife!"—said by a parrot (3:246). The parrot exclaims this numerous times before the enraged Zinoviev finally kills the bird by hurling its cage into a corner (364). Olga, upon hearing the parrot's ominous exclamation, declares that her husband Urbenin will kill her; after Zinoviev kills Olga, he implicates Urbenin in the murder. (In Lermontov's play, *The Masquerade*, a man named Arbenin does kill his wife out of jealousy.) Zinoviev, finishing the story of his tortured relationship with Olga, likens himself to "a bird, released from a cage" (406). In "The Thief" (1883), a man whose wife has turned against him declares that killing is too good for her—and throws a caged bird into a corner, killing it (2:109).

In *My Life* (1896), Misail recalls shooting birds with buckshot in his youth and hearing them groan in a cage at night (9:209). He also recalls how someone's

> . . . green parrot flew out of its cage, and then this beautiful bird wandered about the town for a whole month, lazily flying across from garden to garden, lonely and homeless. Marya Viktorovna reminded me of this bird. (236)

Here, the Russian verb *pereletaya* ("flying across") also suggests bird migration. After they are married, Marya leaves Misail and pursues her singing. When he sees her again, she resembles ". . . a bird that has finally burst out of its cage and adjusts its wings in freedom." (264) Leaving for America, she writes to Misail, declaring that it was a mistake to become his wife and asking him "to correct our mutual mistake, to remove this one stone from my wings" (271). As the story ends, Marya is still living abroad, recalling the escaped, wandering green parrot, lonely and homeless.

In "A Teacher of Literature" (1889), Nikitin loves Masha passionately, but he does not like her dogs, cats, and "the Egyptian pigeons that groaned despondently in a large cage on the terrace." (8:313) Arguing with Masha's sister Vera, Nikitin habitually seizes his head, ". . . running from corner to corner with a groan. And so it was now: he jumped up, seized his head, and walked around the table with a groan." (315) Nikitin's own habitual groaning and trapped behavior tend to associate him with the caged birds. Indeed, he soon describes Masha's house as: "A house in which only Egyptian pigeons groan, and even they do so because they cannot otherwise express their joy!" (318)

After his marriage to Masha, Nikitin's role of a bird, groaning in its cage is further developed as, disillusioned, he seeks refuge in his study to avoid insulting or hitting his wife. More and more, he suspects that being a teacher of literature had never been his calling. The seed for this painful admission was planted by Shebaldin, who was shocked that Nikitin had never read Lessing. Nikitin then had a dream in which he saw birds' nests: "One nest started shaking; Shebaldin peered out of it and cried out loudly: 'You haven't read Lessing!'" (319) After his marriage, Nikitin vividly recalls Shebaldin's head pronouncing this indictment (330)—just as, increasingly often, he shuts himself up in his study: Shebaldin's role as a bird appropriately complements his own.

As we have seen, the separately caged lovers in "The Lady with the Little Dog" are likened in their adultery to "migratory" birds. In "Agafya" (1886), a married woman visits the peasant Savka. Before she arrives, Savka pipes a bird call, and a corncrake answers (5:27). The narrator observes that "during migration, a corncrake does not fly, but runs along the ground." It only flies across rivers and seas, he adds. This impresses Savka, and the narrator discusses migration at some length. Upon hearing that birds feel more at home in "our region," Savka expresses great interest, adding that both birds and people are interesting creatures. Then he rather abruptly declares: "Ekh, sir, if I'd known you'd be coming, I'd never have told that woman to come here."

Soon they hear Agafya, wading across the stream towards Savka's "region." Like the corncrake, she is answering his "call." Also like the corncrake, she is "migrating" by foot, except that she does so even across water. Agafya evidently feels "more at home" in Savka's "region," for she purposely remains there so long that detection, and cruel punishment, become inevitable.

In *The Duel* (1891), Laevsky has a protracted affair with the married Nadezhda Fyodorovna. On the eve of the duel itself, he likens himself to "a migratory bird," seeking salvation in a change of location (7:438). In *Drama At The Hunt*, the people at Olga's wedding party resemble ". . . a flock of storks that had descended to the ruins of an abandoned castle at twilight on one of their days of migration." (3:320) She then leaves her wedding party and commits adultery with Zinoviev in a cave in the garden.[2] When they emerge, he attempts to persuade her to leave her husband: "I spoke eloquently, and not without good reason (*nedarom*) did a female eagle which flew by over our heads flap her wings at me." (327) Shortly thereafter, Count Karneev notices "a little feather" on Zinoviev's coat.

In Chekhov's play *The Three Sisters* (1901), Tuzenbach ruminates on the mysterious laws governing the flight of "migratory birds, cranes for example" (13:147). He addresses his words to Vershinin, who, though married, has recently told Masha (also married) that he loves her. Masha is deeply affected by Tuzenbach's words, and declares that it is very difficult to live without knowing why cranes fly. Vershinin soon tells Masha of a man who was put in prison and only then—as he looked out his prison window—began to be aware of birds (149). (This can be compared to the cages at the end of "The Lady with the Little Dog.") Finally, near the end of the play, Masha associates the departure of "migratory birds" with the departure of Vershinin (178).[3]

In *Three Years* (1895), when Laptev questions Yulia's motives in marrying him, she answers somewhat sadly and quite touchingly—whereupon he abruptly kisses her foot. She then endures his caresses, it seems to him, as an unavoidable consequence of her mistaken marriage: "And she folded the foot he had kissed under herself like a bird. He became sorry for her." (9:60) The next morning, it seems to Laptev that Yulia "stepped uncertainly on the foot that he had kissed."

In "Rothschild's Fiddle" (1894), as Yakov's wife nears death and he realizes in horror how he has abused her for so many years, he sees her: bent, thin and sharp-nosed, "with her mouth open like the profile of a bird that needs to drink" (8:299)—an image that haunts him just before he dies (304). The description is particularly apt because one of the ways he had abused her was to save money by making her drink water instead of tea.

In "Ariadne" (1895), Shamokhin memorably sums up his relationship with the title figure: when Ariadne was with him, he declares, "I felt a coldness in the air, and when she spoke to me of love, I seemed to hear the singing of a metallic nightingale." (9:112) And in "The Spouse" (1895), a man who has detected his wife's unfaithfulness recalls that ". . . a bird would accidentally fly into the house from the yard and begin beating itself furiously against the window-panes and overturning things; so too this woman, from a completely alien environment, had flown into his life and wrought utter havoc there." (9:95)

As one could expect, Chekhov's use of bird images in *The Seagull* (1896) is both far-reaching and complex. Nina Zarechnaya (whose name suggests "beyond the river") quite obviously resembles the girl in Trigorin's idea for a short story:

> ". . . a young girl has lived on the shore of a lake since childhood, a young girl like you. Like a seagull, she loves the lake; and she is happy and free as a seagull. But a man comes along, sees her, and, out of sheer idleness, destroys her, like this seagull here." (13:31–2)

Trigorin's imagined story obviously relates to Nina and ominously anticipates her fate. However, it was Treplev who had shot the bird to which Trigorin refers, placed it at Nina's feet, and declared that he would kill himself in the same way (27). When he does so, at the end of the play, the shot rings out just as Trigorin repeatedly exclaims "I don't remember!" (referring to his order that the dead seagull be stuffed). Not long before, Trigorin had repeated the same words (also about the stuffed seagull), whereupon Treplev had opened the window, saying that he felt an inexplicable restlessness (55). Soon Nina knocked at the window; Treplev admitted her, attributing his restlessness to a premonition that she would come. Yet it is his second, and successful, suicide attempt that coincides with the replay of Trigorin's indifference to the seagull. We are thus simultaneously reminded—via the stuffed seagull—of Trigorin's indifference to Nina and of hers to Treplev at the climax of the play. In "An Every-day Trifle" (1886), a young boy stares pensively at a stuffed bird as he ponders his own and his mother's unhappiness (5:320); separated from her husband, she is having a "long and boring affair" (317). In *The Seagull*, between Trigorin's twin admissions that he fails to remember the stuffed bird, Nina repeatedly calls herself a seagull and reminds Treplev of the seagull he had shot.

In *Drama At The Hunt*, Olga intently watches the struggles of a stint that has been shot "as if she was waiting for its death" (3:358). Zinoviev, who is passionately jealous of her marriage to Urbenin and subsequent cohabitation with Karneev, suggests that she is heartless to observe the stint's sufferings so indifferently. "Others suffer; it can suffer too," she answers. Zinoviev then "finishes off" the bird, and soon he fatally stabs Olga.

Leonid Grossman has singled out from Chekhov's letters a description of

> . . . spring migration in Melikhovo when Isaac Levitan shot down a young woodcock, and Chekhov had to finish him off with a rifle butt; Chekhov's usual identification of man with a wounded animal is strikingly evident here. . . . The wounded woodcock with its bloodied wing and madly astonished eyes rose before him as an eternally sad symbol of human fate.[4]

In *Drama At The Hunt*, before Olga dies, she says that Zinoviev "killed." (378) He quickly suggests that she means "killed the stint," and she dies without naming her murderer.[5] Early in "The Unnecessary Victory" (1882), Arthur shoots a young female eagle that falls into Ilka's lap (1:290); Ilka later marries Arthur, but she has "no regrets" about leaving him before she kills herself at the end of the story.

"The Huntsman" (1885) depicts a meeting between the peasant

Pelageya and her husband Egor. Even though he had beaten and abandoned her, Pelageya caresses him with her gaze. When they meet, Egor is
carrying a "crumpled grouse" in a game bag (4:79). Pelageya lovingly asks
him to stop by and see her "just once." He is her master, she explains,
adding: "Oh, you've shot a grouse." Egor tells her that there can be "no
love of any kind" between them. (He is evidently having an affair with
another woman.)

As he talks with his wife, Egor watches three wild ducks fly past,
become three dots, and disappear in the distance. The huntsman's attention
then shifts "from the ducks to Pelageya," whose fond glimpses of his
gradual disappearance in the distance end the story. The parallel effect is
particularly touching because her face had shone with radiant joy upon
meeting him with his "crumpled grouse."[6]

In Chekhov's often sad and dreary world, one encounters suggestions
that human beings could grow wings and fly. Birds are plentiful in
Chekhov's works,[7] and he frequently used images of birds to depict the
human condition: vulnerable and weak, but capable of rising above ruinous
situations. Chekhov's female characters are likened to birds more often
than are his male characters. With women, the effects are relatively more
serious, more subtle, and more complex. Indeed, Chekhov sometimes likened his male characters to birds for what seems mainly comic effect—for
example, a man whose marriage proposal has just been rejected resembles
"a wet hen."[8] As we have seen, Chekhov favored three types of "passion-
related" bird images, each of which has a generally consistent artistic
function. Caged birds suggest a difficult or uncomfortable relationship
between men and women. Bird migration is associated with adultery or
leaving one's mate. The shooting of birds is linked with doomed passion
or unrequited love; usually, the women's sufferings are associated with
those of the birds. A fateful note is sounded when the characters, for
instance Nina in *The Seagull* and Marya in *My Life,* seem destined to
imitate the birds to which they are likened.

Notes

1. In some cases, birds seem to understand human beings and even to sympathize with
their situations. See, for example, 6:36; 9:315; and 10:159, where larks sing ubiquitously
as if to celebrate the relief of a person, who then seems to become a lark.

Moreover, various birds utter human-like words, and in two short sketches birds actually converse like people. See 5:27; 8:17; 9:332; 10:172–3; and 3:78–9; 10:239–40, respectively.

In his youth, Chekhov caught and sold birds.

2. Moreover, birds raise a clamorous chorus suggesting "migration" just before Olga, who has left her husband to live with Karneev, is murdered by Zinoviev (357).

3. Chebutykin compares himself to an aging "migratory bird" who can no longer fly (175) shortly before he tells Masha that he had loved her mother very much. Richard Peace has noted that Chebutykin's description seems to derive from Pushkin's reference to a disabled crane in *The Gipsies*. Chekhov, Peace adds, had originally written "crane" instead of "migratory bird." As we have seen, Tuzenbach, in his rumination on mysterious laws, had said "migratory birds, cranes for example," so Peace's speculation seems still more valid. See Richard Peace, *Chekhov: A Study of the Four Major Plays* (New Haven, 1983), p. 172.

4. Leonid Grossman, "The Naturalism of Chekhov," Trans. Robert Louis Jackson, *Chekhov: A Collection of Critical Essays*, ed. Robert Louis Jackson (Englewood Cliffs, N.J., 1967), p. 34.

5. Olga's maiden name is Skvortsova ("starling"), and when Zinoviev meets her, he notices that her father has a bird-like face (287). He then sees her in a holiday crowd, where she resembles "a bird, firmly clenched in a fist" (297). Count Karneev, with whom Olga lives before she is murdered, has a body like a "corncrake" (255), and he swaggers like a "young turkey" (343) when he comes between Olga and her husband.

6. In "An Empty Incident" (1886), a woman's question "What pleasure is there in killing birds?" (5:307) seems to reflect her unrequited love.

Discussing the victimization of women in Chekhov's works, Leonid Grossman has observed: "At the very best, woman resembles a wounded bird gazing with silent amazement at the cruel tortures of life." (Grossman, p. 35.)

7. Concerning the numerous birds that appear in the backgrounds of Chekhov's works, I offer the following speculative observations:

Larks (*zhavoronki*) and sparrows (*vorob'i*) usually appear at happy moments and celebrations; the former are frequently associated with weddings and thoughts of marriage (for example, 9:125).

Jackdaws (*galki*) tend to appear in the backgrounds of, or preludes to, unpleasant or embarrassing incidents; starlings (*skvortsy*) and rooks (*grachi*) seem to have ominous or menacing associations (for instance, 9:241, 312). Crows (*vorony*), corncrakes and landrails (*korosteli, dergachi*) also seem generally "negative." Hens and roosters (*kuritsy, petukhi*) are lightly humorous and sometimes faintly ominous as well; see "The Darling" (10:104) and *In The Ravine* (10:149).

Perhaps predictably, geese (*gusi*) seem rather silly (one goose actually spoils a marriage proposal—1:134), and nightingales (*solov'i*) serve as backgrounds for poignant amorous relationships, except when they are humorously mocked as "essential" for this purpose (see 1:104,202) or, in one instance, rendered coldly indifferent by the adjective "metallic" (9:112).

8. This is the Doctor in *Drama At The Hunt* (3:336). The "he" in "He and She" (1882) resembles, in his frockcoat, "a wet jackdaw with a dry tail" (1:241). In "The Crow" (1885),

the hero becomes dead drunk with a prostitute and asks: "Who am I? A pershon? I'm a crow!" (3:434) In "The Commotion" (1886), a man who has just stolen his wife's jewelry "clucks like a hen" (4:332). In "Oh, Women, Women!" (1884), a man "pouts like a turkey" when his love poems are rejected for publication (2:342). And in "Volodya" (1887), a student declares his passion for an older married woman, but she scornfully replies: "Ugh, what a vile duckling!" (6:205)

2

Chekhov's Projecting Images

Anton Chekhov's famous declaration that a rifle hanging on the wall early in a literary work must subsequently fire recommends economy and relevance, but it also suggests a third characteristic of his own writing. As readers or spectators, we tend to anticipate the utilization of that suspended rifle; the shock of its eventual firing is, in a sense, satisfyingly familiar. Chekhov's technique of repeating a few key details near the end of a work—which could be caricatured as, say, "her large brown curls, tiny sparkling eyes, and the yellow flowers on her dress no longer seemed to offer him hope and happiness"—functions quite similarly. Viewed in a different light, the repeated image is both fresh and familiar. Chekhov also produced pairs of images with analogous elements which, as we detect their similarity, often cause the first image to seem faintly projected upon the second.

Chekhov's creative interest in projections can be traced back to his somewhat Gogolian story "Before the Wedding,"[1] published in October of 1880. Much of the tale offers us a view of what will probably happen *after* the wedding—first, through the sorry situation of the young girl's parents, then through the ominous attitude of her fiancé. These suggestive pictures are clearly intended to be seen as projections, for the story ends: "What happened after the wedding, I trust, is discernible not merely to prophets and somnambulists." (1:50)

In "Whose Fault is It?" (1886), a male kitten deemed inept at catching mice is repeatedly abused and even beaten beside a mousetrap for the purpose of instruction (5:460). Having matured, the cat is about to become amorous with a female cat when the appearance of a mouse causes him to bristle, quake, and flee. "Like the kitten," the narrator declares, "I had the honor in my time to be taught Latin by my uncle." And now, upon exposure to the works of classical antiquity, he adds, "I turn pale, my hair stands on end, and, like the cat, I shamefully flee." In "Vanka" (1886), the story of a nine-year-old cobbler's apprentice, the projecting image involves a dog called Vyun. The dog's hind legs, we are told, "had often been damaged by blows; he'd been hanged about two times, was beaten half to death every week, but always came back to life." (5:479) Later, when the much-abused boy writes to his grandfather that his life is "worse than any dog's" (481), we can infer that Vanka, like Vyun, will painfully survive.

"A Confession" (1883) opens by focusing upon the carefree pleasure induced by a clear, frosty day—an emotion compared to the joy of a coachman who has been paid "a gold coin by mistake" (2:26). The narrator, it develops, is ecstatic over his promotion to cashier. As he is then bullied into embezzling funds for his relatives, the phrase "by mistake" acquires an ironic relevance, while the "gold coin" projects as the "gold" (28) with which the already doomed cashier adorns his wife. In "The Death of A Clerk" (1883), the story of a man who worries himself to death after besplattering a general's bald head in the theater, the fateful sneeze is described as follows: "he suddenly made a wry face, his eyes rolled, his breathing stopped" (2:164). This vivid image ultimately projects upon the terse ending: "he lay down on the divan and . . . died."

"He Understood!" (1883) is the tale of a peasant caught poaching on a nobleman's land. Awaiting his fate, he sees a wasp in the room, prevented by the windowpane from escaping. "Why doesn't the fool fly out the door?" he wonders. (2:170) The peasant then realizes that he too, "like the wasp, which keeps falling, now and again, from the glass, will not soon get out of here." Interrogated by the nobleman, he repeatedly fails to explain that an irresistible desire had caused him to poach. At last, he likens his desire to a need to drink, and the nobleman, whose reddish-purple nose signals his receptiveness to the analogy, releases him. He also opens the window, freeing the wasp, and as the story ends, the wasp and the peasant are said to celebrate their freedom. In his vain attempts to explain his motivation, the captive peasant had again resembled the captive wasp, who repeatedly flew into the glass while the door was open.

In "Superfluous People" (1886), Zaikin arrives at his summer dacha to find only his little son Petya. The boy asks why mosquitoes' stomachs become red when they bite (5:199). "Because they suck blood," Zaikin answers. Soon after this, the boy asks why mosquitoes suck blood, whereupon Zaikin "suddenly feels something heavy rise up inside him and begin to suck his liver." His wife later returns with two men—an actor and a singer whom she entertains with food and vodka even though Zaikin complains that he is short of money. The party is loud and late. Finally, the guests spend the night: father and son are moved to Zaikin's study. "Papa, why don't mosquitoes sleep at night?" Petya asks. "Because... because ..." Zaikin mutters, "you and I are superfluous people here."

In "The Plotters" (1887), two gentlemen arrive to eat at the inn of a small town and make mysterious calculations on a sheet of paper. As the reader soon realizes, they are anticipating a solar eclipse, which the ignorant townsfolk take for a supernatural disaster somehow related to the gentlemen's esoteric plotting. Before the eclipse, we are told that a local official later inspected the figures on the plotters' sheet of paper and exclaimed: "Dark is the water in the clouds!" (6:287) In context, this biblical reference[2] humorously confirms that the murky significance of the figures is beyond the local inhabitants' grasp. However, the official's words also project to reinforce the incipient eclipse: ". . . the sky and the ground began to grow dark, as if from an approaching thunderstorm." (288) Two other comic details project. At the inn, one gentleman speaks French, of which the local people "remember only the word 'koshon'" (287). Then, during the eclipse, a terrified man abandons a cartload of cucumbers, which are devoured by pigs (289). Also at the inn, one gentleman complains about his soup and is told by the waiter not to worry: "the cockroaches don't bite." (287) Another effect of the eclipse is that: "The bedbugs in the rooms of the inn, imagining that night had arrived, crawled out of their crevices to set about biting sleepers." (289)

In "The Night Before The Trial" (1886), a man en route to be tried for bigamy makes playful advances to a woman at the station until he discovers that her husband is also present. Having pretended to be a doctor, he continues his charade by writing the woman a ridiculous prescription. In court the next day, the woman's husband turns out to be the prosecutor. "I'll get a bath now!" (*Nu, byt' bane!*) the sham doctor thinks (3:123). Especially in the Russian, this echoes the story's opening words—the coachman's exclamation, upon seeing a hare cross the road, that "There will be misfortune, sir!" (*Byt', barin, bede!*) He says this to the imputed bigamist, who later signs his ridiculous prescription "Dr. Hares" (*D-r Zaitsev*). The first half of the prescription features the Latin phrase "Thus passes worldly fame"—a notion that aptly projects upon the story's ending. The remainder of the prescription, a Latin-disguised recommendation that the woman drink water, can be related to the glass of water downed by her stupified husband upon recognizing the defendant as the sham doctor. The opening "hare" superstition thus humorously seems to deflate the narrator's "worldly fame" in both his roles—as the "Dr. Hares" who makes nocturnal advances and as a presumably convicted bigamist.

Early in "Zinochka" (1887), a young governess teaches a boy three lessons: we inhale oxygen and exhale carbon dioxide; the dangerous Dog Cavern near Naples contains carbon dioxide; "horizon" signifies an apparent merging of ground and sky. Zinochka then absent-mindedly applies the definition of horizon to "Dog Cavern" and leaves the boy to study. Suspicious, he follows and watches her join his older brother Sasha beside a pond: "Zinochka, as if chased into the Dog Cavern and forced to breathe carbon dioxide, walked towards him, barely moving her legs, breathing heavily, with her head thrown back . . ." (6:325) The boy then observes their passionate actions, some of which are described indirectly: "The hill behind which the sun was setting, two willows, the green shores, the sky—all this together with Sasha and Zinochka was reflected in the pond." In this merging of sky and ground, an implicit projection of the boy's third lesson follows explicit evocations of the first two. A particularly nice touch is that Zinochka's mental image of her imminent rendezvous with Sasha had caused her humorous confusion of the dangerous cavern with the concept of horizon, both of which are then projected upon the rendezvous itself.

In the last several stories discussed, the projected images can be seen to occur in groups of three: for example, Petya's three questions in "Superfluous People" and the three lessons in "Zinochka." In Chekhov's early novel *Drama At The Hunt* (1884), a man submits to a publisher a manuscript that begins with three exclamations: "The husband killed his wife! Akh, how stupid you are! Give me some sugar at last!" (3:246) These are merely a parrot's mutterings, learned from a former owner, but each of the three exclamations rather mysteriously projects upon what follows. The first two are relatively straightforward: the author of the thinly-disguised autobiographical manuscript finally tells the publisher that the authorities were "stupid" (415) to believe, eight years ago, that Urbenin killed his wife Olga. The real murderer was the author/hero himself; his manuscript is thus a veiled confession. The parrot's third exclamation ("Give me some sugar at last!") can be seen to project upon the strange author's eight-year-old need to have the satisfaction of being recognized as the extraordinary person he considers himself (414).

In "Gusev" (1890), a man who dies at sea is sewn up in sailcloth and released overboard to meet the open jaws of a shark. Before he dies, Gusev has three delirious memories of his native village, each of which faintly anticipates his burial at sea. And at the very end, the clouds form three images, each of which can be seen to project backwards into the story.

The cloud shapes are a triumphal arch, a lion, and a pair of scissors. The last image clearly suggests the jaws of the shark that has just approached Gusev's body. As the story began, he had spoken of a large fish that made a hole in the bottom of a boat—an unwitting anticipation of this shark. Gusev then suggested that the wind is a "beast" chained to "thick stone walls" near the end of the earth (7:327–8). The cloud images of triumphal arch and lion can be seen to represent this concept.

Thinking of chains and enormous fish, Gusev lapses into his first delirious recollection. He pictures "a huge pond, covered over with snow" and sees his brother and two children riding in a sleigh. Suddenly, and for no apparent reason, the pond is replaced by "the large head of a bull without eyes" (328). This image anticipates the shark, just as the pond and sleigh can be seen to represent the sea and ship. All three images recur in Gusev's second delirious recollection (331). In the third, he pictures himself riding "across the pond," whereupon the sleigh overturns and he flies headlong into a snowdrift, becoming "all white" (334–5). At the end, Gusev's dead body flies downwards headfirst, and as foam covers him, "he seems wrapped in lace" (338).[3]

In "Enemies" (1887), as Abogin brings a doctor home to see his sick wife, we are told that the clouds seemed to be watching over the moon "from all sides, guarding it so that it would not leave" (6:37). Arriving, Abogin learns that his wife, who had feigned illness, has departed with her lover. He then curses the servants for allowing her to leave, and Chekhov remarks that the moon had already left the clouds "which were guarding it" (43). The same Russian verb is used for the wife's leaving and in both descriptions of the departing moon.[4]

In "The Peasants" (1897), the young girl Sasha is flogged by her grandmother for failing to keep the geese out of the kitchen-garden. Falling asleep that night, Sasha imagines ". . . the terrible judgment: a big stove, like a kiln, was burning, and the Unclean Spirit, all black, with horns like a cow's, was chasing Granny into the fire with a long stick, as she herself had recently chased the geese." (9:294) The scene imagined by the punished girl explicitly echoes a previous one, but it also projects forward in two different ways. First, a fire breaks out at night in a peasant's hut after an old man who "resembles a gnome" and on whose bald head the flames are reflected (295) arrives from another village. (Upon his arrival, a samovar was moved, and the straw roof caught fire.) After this, Sasha's grandmother becomes furious when their own samovar is appropriated, for nonpayment of taxes, by the village elder, who is later seen soldering something "beside a stove" and said to be "entirely black" and to resemble "a sorcerer" (304). The elder is thus a still more precise projection of vengeful Sasha's Unclean Spirit, and it seems appropriate that Granny shrieks and pursues him when he takes the samovar.[5] Like the coachman's "hare" superstition ("The Night Before The Trial"), the narrator's idea of a "gold coin mistake" ("A Confession"), Zinochka's confusion of the Dog Cavern and "horizon," the official's notion of dark water in the clouds ("The Plotters"), and Gusev's delirious recollections, Sasha's "terrible judgment" has projections that are especially remarkable for having their roots in a character's mental image.

In "The Student" (1894), the recounted story of Peter's betrayal of Christ can be seen to project both forwards and backwards. As Donald Rayfield has observed, several details of the biblical story have a mirror-like relationship with their counterparts elsewhere in Chekhov's tale: the workmen, the campfire, the calling of birds, the "beaten" younger widow and "beaten" Christ, the weeping of Peter and of the older widow, and the dawn and sunset.[6] We are evidently invited to detect these complex relationships, for as the student relates the biblical story, he declares: "Peter stood with them beside the fire and also warmed himself, just as I am now." (8:308)

In *The Seagull* (1896), Trigorin's inspiration for "the plot of a short story" also projects both forwards and backwards: "A young girl like you has lived on the shore of a lake since childhood; she loves the lake like a seagull and is happy and free as a seagull. But a man happens to arrive, sees her, and idly destroys her, just like that seagull there." (13:31–2) In Chapter Ten of *Three Years* (1895), Kostya Kochevoi's objection to literary works wherein "she now loves him but he no longer loves her" functions similarly—especially since Yulia (the "she" at the end of the novel) immediately agrees (9:55). Yulia then adds three other ingredients (a lovers' meeting, a betrayal, and a meeting after a separation) which can also be seen to project outwards, though less clearly. (The third anticipates Laptev and Yulia's meeting at the very end, but the first two seem more pertinent to Laptev and Polina: the flashback to their affair in Chapter Seven and his discovery that she is living with Yartsev in Chapter Fourteen.) In *The Three Sisters* (1901), Masha's repeated quoting of Pushkin's *Ruslan and Lyudmila* suggests her situation in the play, as Richard Peace has shown. In her strength, vigor, an capacity for life, Masha herself resembles the "green oak," bound in marriage by a "golden chain" to the "learned tomcat" Kulygin—a pompous schoolmaster who with his prattle and fussing "round and round" her constantly hems her in. [7]

Also in *The Three Sisters*, Solyony's remark that he may one day put a bullet into Tuzenbach's forehead (13:124) anticipates their duel (and its outcome) at the end of the play. This may remind us of that suspended rifle which, according to Chekhov, must eventually be discharged, and it seems fitting to close with a few projecting images that involve firearms. Early in *The Duel* (1891), Von Koren's habitual, protracted aiming with a pistol at Prince Vorontsov's portrait (7:367) tends to project upon his aiming at Laevsky's forehead in their duel near the end. This seems particularly so because Laevsky's wrathful words—which afford Von Koren the opportunity to accept his "challenge"—are directed towards the portrait of Prince Vorontsov (425). And as Vladimir Nabokov has observed, when Treplev shoots himself at the end of *The Seagull*, his mother imitates her "real" (and, therefore, projected) reaction "by recalling a former occasion." [8]

In "Oversalted" (1885), the firearms suggestively suspended before us are purely imaginary, and their subsequent utilization is imagined as well. Having hired a peasant to drive him at night across desolate terrain, an official becomes frightened and lies that he has "three revolvers" with him (4:214). He later elaborates on this lie, claiming that four friends are planning to meet him on the way, "each with a pistol," whereupon the peasant abandons him, convinced that the official is planning to steal his horse and cart. The title of the story, *Peresolil* (figuratively, "Went Too Far"), obviously refers to the embellished lie, but it also anticipates an earlier, and projecting, image. At first, the peasant's horse must be beaten several times before it will even move, but later it runs so fast through the woods that "there is no way to stop it." (215) This causes the frightened official to elaborate on his firearm story: the unstoppable horse inspires the runaway lie.

Unlike the narrator of "Oversalted," Anton Chekhov did not overdo his effects. Even when their analogous elements are explicitly acknowledged, Chekhov's projecting images seem neither exaggerated nor inappropriately obvious. Remarkably often, the projecting images involve animals of all sorts—from cats and dogs to birds and insects. Perhaps the most pleasing and startling projections are those with their origins in the mental images of Chekhov's characters. The more complex patterns typically comprise a cluster of three images, each of which may project forwards or backwards within a given work. The more subtle forward projections evoke in the reader or spectator a strategically delayed blending of satisfied anticipation and surprise, while enriching the texture of Chekhov's ostensibly uncomplicated art.

Notes

1. Apart from the humorously unoptimistic outlook on marriage, Gogolisms include the strategic vagueness used to describe the two young people, the parents' faces which are not faces at all, and the kiss planted by the groom upon the lower lip of Miss Back-of-the-heady (Podzatylkina).

2. See Chekhov, 6:681.

3. The prophetic pond in "Gusev" can be considered a distant relation of the pond wherein the hero of "Neighbors" (1892) discerns "terrible pictures of the future." (8:71)

4. *Ushla!* (three times, p. 39) and *ushyol* (37, 43).

In *The Seagull*, Chekhov has Trigorin parody *Hamlet* by insisting that a cloud resembles a piano (13:29). Trigorin then declares that he must not fail to mention a floating piano-shaped cloud in his writing; later, Treplev deems his own writing—characterized by "the distant sounds of a piano, dying away in the quiet, fragrant air" (55)—inferior to Trigorin's.

5. However, the gnome-like man appears again as the story ends, with the sun reflected on his bald head.

6. Donald Rayfield, *Chekhov: The Evolution of his Art* (New York, 1975), p. 154.

7. Richard Peace, *Chekhov: A Study of the Four Major Plays* (New Haven, 1983), pp. 78–80.

8. Vladimir Nabokov, *Lectures on Russian Literature*, ed. Fredson Bowers (New York, 1981), p. 295.

3

Chekhov's Emotional Green Focus

Chekhov's reputation as the painter of a gloomy, twilight Russia may be somewhat unjustified.[1] Yet the world of his works does seem predominantly gray. In Vladimir Nabokov's view, Chekhov managed to convey artistic beauty "by keeping all his words in the same dim light and of the same exact tint of gray."[2] One might therefore not expect to find a patterned appearance of any other color. As we shall see, however, a focusing on greenness tends to accompany—or even to highlight—intense emotional experiences in Chekhov's works. Contrary to what one might expect, these "green-focused" episodes usually involve pain, separation, and death.

In *The Duel* (1881), two green rays of light appear in the sky at sunrise just prior to the duel itself (7:443). Chekhov then uses these rays to suggest the feelings of the two antagonists. Von Koren, who excitedly calls attention to the rays, tries to conceal his agitation by "pretending that the green rays interested him more than anything else." Laevsky is said to feel awkward and conspicuous, like a man who may soon die. He views "the green rays" and the people at the duel as "utterly disconnected with the night he has just lived through," in which his life and his relationship with Nadezhda became so much more meaningful.

Von Koren exclaims that he is seeing the green rays for "the first time in my life!" Laevsky, we are told, was seeing a sunrise for "the first time in his life." These two phrases ironically suggest that death may be imminent, and the unusual green rays add an appropriate coolness to the warmth of the morning sun.

The green rays in *The Duel* may be related to the "wide green ray" (7:339) that appears in the sky after Gusev's burial at sea ("Gusev," 1890), but their artistic function is closer to that of the green lamps in "The House with the Mezzanine" and in "Sleepy."[3]

"The House with the Mezzanine" (1896) is narrated by the landscape painter N., who describes his and Zhenya's realization, beneath some shooting stars, that they love each other. Having accompanied her home, he remains outside: the house seems to look at him with the "eye-like" windows of its mezzanine (where Zhenya sleeps) as if it understood everything (9:189). As N. watches, however, these windows turn green (a lamp was being covered by a green shade).[4] After about an hour, the green light goes out, and it becomes very cold. As he realizes the next morning, Lida, to whom Zhenya told "everything," had forbidden her to see N. again. Their painful separation is thus associated with the greening of the light—and with the coldness that followed. Concluding his story, N. declares that he sometimes recalls the green light in the windows, and how he had walked home, deeply in love, rubbing his hands from the cold.

In "Sleepy" (1888), the young servant girl Varka is driven beyond her endurance by overwork and sleeplessness to smother the baby in her charge. Throughout the story, a green lamp casts on the ceiling a flickering green spot that seems to come to life. The green spot gradually establishes a rapport with Varka, "winking"[5] at her and "sneaking" into her half-open eyes. Finally, as Varka stealthily approaches the baby's cradle, she laughs, winks, and threatens the conniving green spot with her finger (7:12).

Aksinya, who purposely scalds a baby to death in Chekhov's novel *In The Ravine* (1900), has eyes that "burn green" (10:160). She wears a green dress with a yellow bosom—Nabokov has suggested that this dress makes her resemble a kind of rattlesnake found in eastern Russia[6]—and she is called "green Aksinya" (155, 156). Before the murder, the baby's mother fearfully notices the anger in Aksinya's burning green eyes.[7]

In "The Avenger" (1887) a cuckolded husband, pondering revenge, prices revolvers in a shop. At last, he decides it will be safer to punish the lovers with a divorce scandal, but feels he ought to purchase something from the attentive clerk. His gaze comes to rest upon a "green net" hanging near the door. (6:333) Learning that it is "a net to catch quail," he buys it and, "feeling himself still more insulted," departs. Having caught his wife with her lover, the miserable husband is thus himself "caught" by an obligation to purchase the green net—and shown to be a rather sorry "avenger" as well.

In "The Correspondent" (1882), an old newspaper reporter in a dark-green frock-coat is ridiculed and abused at a wedding party. As the tipsy guests throw him up to the ceiling, they call him a "dark-green scoundrel" (1:182).

In "Rothschild's Fiddle" (1894), when Rothschild asks Yakov to play in the orchestra, Yakov finds it "repulsive to look at Rothschild's green frock-coat" (8:302) and viciously chases him away. Bitten by dogs, Rothschild emits a "desperate, sickly cry." At the end of the story, Yakov again refuses to play but treats the frightened Rothschild "affectionately" and says: "I've taken ill, brother." Then, as the dying Yakov plays his fiddle, Rothschild becomes sorrowfully compassionate: "And tears slowly rolled down his cheeks and dropped upon his green frock-coat." (305) Recalling Rothschild's "desperate cry" (when his green coat had seemed repulsive), Yakov leaves his fiddle to Rothschild.

In "Agafya" (1885), a married peasant woman defiantly remains with her lover Savka. The next morning, as she hesitantly leaves, Savka observes that it must be terrifying to return to her husband. He says this "gazing at the bright green stripe that stretched out behind Agafya in the dewy grass" (5:34). As a focus for Savka's concern, the trail that Agafya is now leaving behind her reminds us that she did so in another sense by overstaying the night before. Her husband knows that she didn't come there to pick cabbages, Savka grimly declares.

Chekhov associated intensely focused greenness with impending punishment in other works, for example in "The Criminal" (1885). Caught unscrewing a nut from a railroad tie to use as a fishing sinker, a peasant utterly fails to understand that this practice could cause a train wreck. Finally, the exasperated investigator commands him to be silent: the peasant stands ". . . staring at the table with the green cloth and intensely blinking his eyes as if he saw before him not the cloth, but the sun." (4:87) This description aptly complements the peasant's blindness to the nature of his crime: threatened by prison, he assumes that his punishment relates to a charge of arrears with the village elder. Somewhat similar episodes can be found in *My Life* (1896), "The Inquiry" (1883), and "The Swedish Match" (1884),[8] but it should be noted that Russian officials commonly sat behind "green tables" in those days.[9] In "Expensive Lessons" (1887), a young man hires a shapely French woman to teach him French. After she leaves, he sits at the table, "stroking the green cloth with his palms" (6:389) and contemplating her need to earn money. His action clearly reflects the turn of his thoughts, which, as the lessons continue, become increasingly erotic.

As one might expect, Chekhov associated the color green in his works with drunkenness and devils. (Nabokov has suggested that the devil seen by Russian drunkards has green blood.[10]) In "The Meeting Took Place, But..." (1882), Gvozdikov arrives for a nocturnal rendezvous hopelessly drunk. Before this, we observe his growing stupor: ". . . he automatically placed a cork on the neck of a bottle and cocked his finger at it, trying to flick it into the little green spot that flashed before his eyes." (1:176) In "Conversation of a Man with a Dog" (1885), a drunken man knocks "a little green devil" from his sleeve (3:187), while in "A Drunk Talks with a Sober Devil" (1886), the devil is covered with green fur, and the drunk recalls that "green devils have the stupid habit of appearing to all drunks generally" (4:338). In "Akh, Teeth!" (1886), a man feels as if "the devil himself with his little imps has settled in his tooth," whereupon everything "turns green before his eyes" (5:332).

Chekhov used a description of "greenness before the eyes" (*zeleneet v glazakh*) in three other works. In "Late-blooming Flowers" (1882) everything "goes green" before Marusya's eyes as she painfully strains to help carry her brother's bed (1:398). In "Kashtanka" (1887), the dog of that name is so cruelly abused that everything "goes green" before her eyes and all her joints ache (6:434). And in the famous ending of *Ward No. 6* (1892), as Doctor Ragin dies from a painful apoplectic stroke: "Everything went green before his eyes." (8:126) Particularly for Chekhov, who was a doctor, the phenomenon of "seeing green" (much as "seeing red" suggests intense anger in English) seems to result from distress so intense that it approaches a loss of consciousness.[11] In some English translations, *zeleneet v glazakh* is rendered as "seeing green spots before one's eyes," and the hypnotic green spot in "Sleepy" (discussed above) that haunts the exhausted servant girl may be considered a protracted enactment of this idiomatic expression. In Russian, "green boredom" (*zelyonaya skuka*) means "intolerable boredom," and to chase someone "along the green street" is to make them "run the gauntlet." Three characters in Chekhov's works have greenish hair— Father Anastasi in "The Letter" (1887); Granny in "The Peasants" (1897); Father Sisoi in "The Bishop" (1902)—and all three descriptions occur in generally unpleasant episodes.[12]

We may conclude that a focusing upon greenness frequently attends the intense emotional experiences of Chekhov's characters. In such cases, the experiences are usually unpleasant ones, involving pain, separation, or death. Most of the green focusings occur (or are recalled) near the end of a given work, providing an atmospheric coloration of the episode that tends to linger in the reader's memory. Images of glowing or shining light provide the most striking effects: rays, spots, eyes, and lamps. Quite often, the details of the green focus reflect the experience itself. In some cases, the characters' emotional sufferings are aggravated by physical exhaustion, sleeplessness, or the overuse of alcohol—suggesting a "sickly" distortion of consciousness. The green focus may thus possibly be related to the Russian expression "seeing green" (*zeleneet v glazakh*) and perhaps even to the alleged greenness of Russian devils.

Notes

1. See Simon Karlinsky, Introduction to *Anton Chekhov's Life and Thought: Selected Letters and Commentary* (Berkeley, 1975), pp. 2–3.

2. Vladimir Nabokov, *Lectures on Russian Literature*, Fredson Bowers, ed. (New York, 1981), p. 253.

3. Donald Rayfield has mentioned that the green lights create a similar effect in the first three of these four works (*Chekhov: The Evolution of his Art*, New York, 1975, pp. 122, 161).

4. In "Vint" (1884), an official watches as his subordinates furtively play cards: "with faces painted green by the lampshades," they seem to resemble "fairytale gnomes or, God forbid, counterfeiters" (3:69). The notion of counterfeiters is particularly appropriate because, as the official soon learns, the truant workers have pasted photographs of important people over the faces of their playing cards. In "The Unusual One" (1886), when a man seeks a midwife at night, her face is "painted green" by "the little lamp with a green shade that she holds in her hands" (5:354).

5. Gleb Struve has observed that different forms of the same Russian verb are used for the spot's "flickering" and for its "winking"—an effect easily lost in translation. ("On Chekhov's Craftsmanship: The Anatomy of a Story," in: Ralph E. Matlaw, ed., *Anton Chekhov's Short Stories*, Norton Critical Edition, New York, 1979, p. 332.)

6. Nabokov, p. 267.

7. In "Strong Feelings" (1886), a lawyer whose "green eyes" make him appear "unhappy, inconsequential and dull" (5:110) persuades the passionate narrator that he is not really in love.

8. Chekhov, 9:234; 2:225, 213.

9. In Tolstoy's novel *Resurrection*, we are told that one such table "was covered not with green cloth" but with cloth of another color (13:280).

Several focusings upon green roofs in Chekhov's works are associated with the sad finality of parting or separation (6:267; 9:260, 342; 10:74, 159), but like the green cloths on officials' tables, green roofs were common in Chekhov's Russia. In *My Life* (1896), some huts are maliciously smeared with green paint (9:224).

10. Vladimir Nabokov, *Nikolai Gogol* (New York, 1944), p. 6.

11. In Dostoevsky's *Poor People*, Varvara Alekseevna uses the expression *v glazakh zelenelo* to describe her condition when she was exhausted from fatigue and lack of sleep (1:111).

12. See Chekhov, 6:154; 9:303; and 10:193, respectively. In "The Baron" (1882), the sad hero has a "green patina" on his bald head, caused by the green lining of his fur cap (1:452).

4

Some Revealing Connections in *Anna Karenina*

In a well-known letter of April 1876, Tolstoy referred to "that endless labyrinth of connections which is the essence of art."[1] He also emphasized the importance of connections in *Anna Karenina,* adding that they "can only be expressed indirectly—by words describing characters, actions, and situations." While tracing patterns of connections in Tolstoy's novel,[2] we shall expose a subtle substructure involving three characters who function in unexpectedly complex ways: Anna's son Seryozha, the peasant nurse Matryona Filimonovna, and Stiva Oblonsky.

Early in the novel, the Oblonsky children play a train game in which passengers fall (8:15). This game prefigures the death of the train watchman, which combines with Frou-Frou's fatal fall to foreshadow Anna's death. In the game, the girl Tanya cries out when the passengers fall; in an earlier version of the novel, Anna was called "Tatyana" and Frou-Frou, its diminutive, "Tanya." In the final version, Tanya is Anna's favorite Oblonsky child (9:200), and Anna sees some children "playing at horses" on the way to her suicide (9:352).

The fact that railroad is "iron road" in Russian enables Tolstoy to establish numerous connections, some of which resist translation into English. The dream that haunts both Vronsky and Anna gradually becomes more explicit until she dreams of a peasant doing something terrible "in iron over her" (9:347). And when she finally throws herself beneath the train, a peasant is said to be "working at the rails" (9:364)—literally, "over the iron." Before the ball, Anna congratulates Kitty about Vronsky, adding that she met him "at the railroad station" (8:85)—literally, "on the iron road." At home, Anna thinks of "what had seemed so meaningful to her on the iron road" (8:125) and tells her husband about the watchman's death "on the iron road" (8:125).

Late in the novel, Anna's son Seryozha describes a train game that foreshadows her death—a game for which he uses the term "iron road" (9:319). Just before this, his father remarks that the boy has been "sea bathing." This links the episode still more closely with Anna's dive beneath the train, which is associated with a feeling of entering the water "while bathing" (9:364–5). As she dives, Anna discards her red handbag; she had recently frowned when speaking of a woman in a red bathing suit and then shaken her head as if driving away an unpleasant thought (9:336). Another apparent link with Tolstoy's earlier plan to have Anna kill herself by drowning is the fact that Vronsky's horse Frou-Frou falls at a water jump, struggling like a fish. Sydney Schultze has discussed these and other images of drowning in the novel.[3]

Just before Seryozha describes his prophetic train game, he becomes disturbed by his uncle Stiva's resemblance to his mother. When Stiva releases his hand, the boy is likened to "a bird set free" (9:318)—a link with the fact that Anna was compared to "a captive bird" when she witnessed Frou-Frou's fatal jump (8:233).[4] Seryozha then observes that in his game, the passengers may fall. As he says the word "fall," Stiva notices that his eyes resemble Anna's and asks him if he remembers her. Deeply disturbed, the boy answers that he does not. Earlier, when told that his mother was dead, Seryozha had refused to believe it, so this response seems somewhat ominous. The boy now becomes so upset that he exclaims "Leave me in peace!" He directed this, Tolstoy tells us, "not to his tutor" (who is talking with him) "but to the entire world" (9:320)—which may be connected with Anna's strangely generalized "No, I won't let you torture me," directed, prior to her suicide, "not to him, not to herself, but to that which was making her suffer" (9:363).

Throughout the novel, the Russian word *obrazuetsya* (something like "things will shape themselves" or "everything will turn out all right") is correctly applied to various troublesome situations.[5] First, as the servant Matthew applies it to the discord between Stiva and Dolly, Stiva answers: "Do you think so? Who's there?" (8:12) It is the nurse Matryona Filimonovna, come to urge Stiva to make peace with Dolly. Strangely enough, we learn only much later that *obrazuetsya* is really Matryona's expression: "Matthew had taken it from her" (8:288). Matryona's interruption is thus

almost eerily timed to promote the effectiveness of her own expression:
Stiva agrees to seek a reconciliation.

When he does so, Dolly's hostility diminishes somewhat, and Stiva
thinks: "Perhaps things will shape themselves [*obrazuetsya*]!" Dolly, alone,
realizes that she still loves Stiva but then begins to recall his unfaithfulness:

> "The most awful thing is that ..." she began, but did not finish her thought because
> Matryona Filimonovna thrust her head in at the door. (8:21)

Once again, Matryona's interruption seems to promote the effect of her own
prophetic expression: her arrival prevents Dolly's thoughts of Stiva from
turning negative. Matryona even provides a helpful distraction by asking
about household affairs, whereupon Dolly "drowned her grief in them for a
while."

When we later learn that *obrazuetsya* is really Matryona's expression,
she applies it to Dolly's problems in the country, and Tolstoy remarks that
Matryona was "an inconspicuous [*nezametnoe*] but most important and most
useful person" in the family. Matryona then arranges for everything to run
smoothly. She even ingeniously remakes the clothes that Tanya wears to
go to church (8:290). This is echoed when Stiva correctly applies
obrazuetsya to Levin's clothing problems before going to church for his
wedding (9:19, 20).

Stiva's use of Matryona's prophetic expression in connection with
Levin's wedding is revealing—especially when combined with another
echo. When Matryona had beneficially interrupted Stiva, Tolstoy told us
that she was "on his side" (8:12)—and when we learn that Dolly has
(correctly) predicted Levin's marriage to Kitty, Stiva tells Levin: "She
is—on your side." (8:47) Now, when Levin visits Dolly in the country, and
she tells him of what Matryona has accomplished after saying *obrazuetsya*,
the peasant woman smiles warmly at Levin. Matryona, Tolstoy explains,
knew Levin and wanted him to marry Kitty (8:294). Soon after this, Dolly
starts speaking about Kitty. Levin abruptly and persistently changes the
subject to matters of farming (8:295–6). But Matryona, Tolstoy tells us, had
Dolly's affairs running smoothly, and so Dolly, deciding to run the farm as
Matryona had advised, persists in speaking about Kitty. This causes a brief
resurrection of hope in Levin's heart (8:297), and before long, he emphatically decides that he loves Kitty (8:306). Tolstoy thus has the "incon-

spicuous" but "most useful" Matryona play a subtle but constantly effective role in promoting her two desired goals: Stiva's reconciliation with Dolly and Levin's marriage to Kitty. In both cases, moreover, her prophetic expression is applied indirectly—by both Matthew and Stiva to Stiva's marriage and by Stiva to Levin's wedding.

Matryona's two goals are also linked in the novel by Stiva and by the unusual image of a "mother-of-pearl shell." After Stiva agrees to seek a reconciliation, he lights a cigarette, takes two puffs, throws it into a "mother-of-pearl shell" ashtray, and goes to Dolly's bedroom (8:16). When Stiva and Levin have dinner, they eat oysters that have a "mother-of-pearl shell" (8:44). Pushing away the empty shells, Stiva asks if Levin plans to visit the Shcherbatskys that evening. (He does, and proposes, but is refused.) Finally, after Stiva has reproached Levin for ceasing to pursue Kitty (8:191), Levin's inspiration to propose to her again is attended by a "strange mother-of-pearl shell" cloud formation in the sky (8:305). In every case, Tolstoy uses the words *perlamutrovaya rakovina*, but English translations routinely obscure the connections.[6]

As the cloud-shell undergoes what is termed a "mysterious" (*tainstven-naya*) transformation, Levin decides that he loves Kitty. Just prior to his successful proposal, we are then told that he and Kitty had "not a conversation, but some sort of mysterious [*tainstvennoe*] communication (8:428).[7] While gazing at the sky late in the novel, Levin seems to hear "mysterious" (*tainstvennye*) voices and concludes that he may have found faith (9:398). Shortly thereafter, he associates the stars with his new beliefs. Kitty suddenly appears and examines his face "by the light of the stars" (9:416). After Kitty had accepted his marriage proposal, Levin stayed awake all night, gazing at the stars (8:441). Early in the novel, Levin had gazed at the stars of the Great Bear and abruptly asked Stiva about Kitty (8:183). At this point, "dim Arcturus" (the guardian of the Bear) was mentioned, suggesting Levin and his interest in Kitty, whom he thought of as "Tiny Bear."[8] Appropriately, then, Levin is said to be "catching and losing" the stars of the Great Bear. The adjective applied to Arcturus, "dim" (*mrachnyj*), commonly means "gloomy" and aptly describes the mood of the "guardian" Levin: he is braced for the news that Kitty has accepted Vronsky. Stiva dispels this fear, but explains that Kitty has been very ill, after which the word *mrachnyj* is indeed applied to Levin four times in the next six pages. It is then that Stiva reproaches Levin for not persisting in his efforts to win Kitty. As he does so, his eyes are said to shine out of his face "like stars" (8:191).[9] At this point, Stiva refers back to their earlier conversation wherein he said that Dolly, a successful prophet of marriages, was "on Levin's side," which, as we have seen, was linked with Matryona's desire that Levin marry Kitty. Curiously, however, Stiva now quotes himself as having said that he did not know "on whose side the chances were greater," whereas he had actually assured Levin that, in his opinion, the chances were "on Levin's side" (8:49). This may be intended to illustrate Stiva's rather fickle nature, but it may also be one of several apparent contradictions in Tolstoy's novel.[10]

After Stiva's early assurance, Levin tells him that he "decidedly" cannot understand how a married man can have an affair, likening it to stealing a "roll" after a full meal (8:50). "Why not?" Stiva replies. "A roll sometimes smells so that one cannot resist." Levin smiles but soon advises Stiva not to "steal rolls." After Kitty accepts Levin's proposal, Levin, who has recently eaten very little food, tries to put a "roll" into his mouth: ". . .but his mouth decidedly did not know what to do with the roll. Levin spat the roll out . . ." (8:441–2) This connection is weakened in English translations, and the echo of "decidedly" (*reshitel'no*) is lost entirely.[11]

Early in the novel, Kitty tells Anna that she envisions her "wearing lilac" at the ball. "Why necessarily lilac?" Anna asks (8:85). At the ball, we see Anna: "not wearing lilac, as Kitty had necessarily desired, but black" (8:91). Kitty, Tolstoy repeats, had pictured her "necessarily wearing lilac," but now, upon seeing her "wearing black," she "understood that Anna could not have worn lilac." Tolstoy explains that Anna's "black dress" served as an inconspicuous frame for her charm,[12] but he has also established a connection between "wearing lilac or black" and Anna's enticing Vronsky away from Kitty.

At Kitty's wedding, a guest named Marie's wearing "lilac" is said to be inappropriate, like wearing "black" (9:26). This rather strange association—particularly because Levin's half-brother soon thinks of a girl, also named Marie, who died before he could marry her[13] and because of the fear, before Kitty's wedding, that it would be delayed by another woman's death and the ensuing period of mourning (9:7)—may remind us (via the lilac/black echo) that the ball had marked the "death" of Kitty's hopes to marry Vronsky (she was then described as *ubitoyu*, literally, "killed") and, in a sense, the "death" of Anna's own marriage (her son is later told that she herself has "died"). Three additional connections reinforce all this.

When Anna believes that she is dying in childbirth, her midwife wears a hat "with lilac ribbons" (8:450). Then, after Seryozha is told that his mother has "died" (9:88), it is explained to the boy that she "has died for him because she is bad" (9:102); in the next sentence, we read that Seryozha's heart skipped a beat when he saw a woman "in a lilac veil,"[14] expecting that it was his mother—and Anna *is* described as wearing a veil both when she visits him (9:111) and just before her death (9:361). In addition, Anna becomes painfully jealous of Vronsky and someone twice described as a "girl in a lilac hat" (9:347). He then says "Anna, it's impossible to live like this," and she tells him that he will "repent," a word that the expression on the face of her corpse later seems to him to be pronouncing (9:378). Descriptions of "women in black and lilac" thus link Anna's captivation of Vronsky with its dual consequences of her near death and death. In Tolstoy's *Sevastopol Stories,* as Praskukin dies, he has a vision of a woman in a hat "with lilac ribbons" (2:133), and the wording matches the description of Anna's midwife (*v cheptse c lilovymi lentami*).

When Anna returns home early in the novel, Seryozha tells his governess: "I told you it was mama! I knew!" (8:122) This seems natural enough in context, especially since the boy may have rationalized the precision of his expectation. Even when he later repeats his "I knew" four times when Anna returns on his birthday (9:113–4), it may seem quite natural. As both Tolstoy (9:102) and Seryozha (9:114) insist, however, the boy had never believed in her death, even when it was announced to him by Lydia Ivanovna and "confirmed" by his father (9:102). Moreover, as we have seen, Seryozha's train game prefigures Anna's death, and when the game is described, he somewhat ominously reverses his attitude to pretend that he does not remember her.

Returning to Seryozha's "knowing" that his mother would return on his birthday, we find that it was a "secret" for which he had been "praying" and which, he declared, he could "see more clearly without a candle" (9:106). Tolstoy then writes:

> When the candle had been taken away, Seryozha heard and felt his mother. She was standing over him and caressing him with a loving look. But windmills appeared, and a little knife, and everything got mixed up, and he fell asleep.

The last two images quite obviously derive from Seryozha's making "windmills" (9:105) and from the "little knife" he played with as the chapter began (9:102). While playing with the little knife, however, Seryozha had thought about his mother, refusing to believe her dead, which, in context, led to a description of his brief, heart-stopping hope that he had glimpsed her wearing a lilac veil, which, as we have seen, was prophetically linked with Anna's death. Moreover, since the images of "windmills" and "little knife" intrude upon the child's prophetic vision of Anna's return (to stand over his bed and caress him), this intrusion may be connected with the fact that both images are destructive in Anna's own life. Just before meeting Vronsky on the train platform in the snowstorm, Anna had repeatedly handled a "little knife" (for cutting book pages), pressing its "smooth and cold surface to her cheek" (8:115). As Edward Wasiolek has observed: "The knife may be taken as a detail signifying the destructive possibility of the passion, especially in a context that is manifestly sexual."[15] The other image, the "windmills," is directly connected with Anna's destructive affair, but this is lost in English translations. Speaking to Anna, and obviously with her in mind, Princess Betsy remarks that affairs have become the latest fashion for everyone: "They have thrown their bonnets beyond the windmills." (8:328) This is a Russian translation of the French expression *"jeter son bonnet par-dessus les moulins,"* used to describe women who defy social opinion.[16] Another connection is that Princess Betsy again uses the same expression with Anna just two pages after Seryozha's vision of the windmills. Moreover, she uses it in predicting the social censure awaiting Anna—a contributing factor in her suicide.

Many of these intricate connections suggest that Seryozha—unlike the celebrated Landau-Bezzubov—is a genuine "seer." Tolstoy declares in the novel that "dissembling" may deceive the most intelligent adult but not "the most limited child" (8:295). As we have seen, Seryozha's faith and intuition play a surprisingly important role—as do the devotion and inspirations of Matryona Filimonovna. Together, they combine to urge, persistently though often subtly, a Tolstoyan belief in the transcendent goodness and wisdom of children and natural peasant folk. Various other connections suggest that Stiva Oblonsky functions in two quite unexpected ways: to illuminate some of his nephew's intuition and to link Matryona's goal of restoring Stiva's own marriage with her goal of promoting Levin's marriage to Kitty.

Notes

1. R. F. Christian, ed., *Tolstoy's Letters* (New York, 1978), 1:297.

2. English translations of *Anna Karenina* cited will be by: Joel Carmichael (New York,

1978); Constance Garnett (New York, 1966); David Magarshack (New York, 1961); Louise and Aylmer Maude (New York, 1970—Norton Critical Edition).

3. See Sydney Schultze, *The Structure of Anna Karenina* (Ann Arbor, 1982), pp. 116–7.

4. Frou-Frou herself is likened to "a wounded bird" (8:221) just after she falls.

5. See my *Leo Tolstoy* (Boston, 1986), p. 81.

6. The Maudes have: "pearl-shell" (p. 8), "pearly shells" (p. 32), and "strange mother-of-pearl coloured shell" (p. 252). Carmichael has: "mother-of-pearl" (p. 10), "pearly shells" (p. 36), and "strange mother-of-pearl colored shell" (p. 295). Magarshack has: "mother-of-pearl shell-shaped" (p. 25), "pearly shells" (p. 50), and "curious mother-of-pearl shell" (p. 285). Garnett has: "mother-of-pearl" (p. 10), "pearly shell" (p. 39), and "strange mother-of-pearl shell" (p. 306).

7. This same word had been continually applied, early in the novel, to Levin's impressions of Kitty, her family, and love. See my *Nabokov & Others: Patterns in Russian Literature* (Ann Arbor, 1979), p. 56.

8. See Schultze, p. 112.

9. The Maude translation reads, simply, "glittering" (p. 156). Carmichael, Garnett, and Magarshack all include the word "stars" (pp. 181, 189, 183, respectively).

10. As Vladimir Nabokov has pointed out in *Pnin*, it is not clear whether *Anna Karenina* begins on Friday (8:20) or on Thursday (8:41). Moreover, Tolstoy's description of the steeplechase course (8:217–8) is quite different from the jumps and obstacles he describes during the race. There is also some apparent confusion about whether Karenin touches his hat (8:391) or bows (8:395) to Vronsky upon meeting him in the doorway. And Kitty, whose face lights up with "joyous amazement" in a carriage as she "recognizes" Levin (8:305), is "amazed" (8:420) when Levin reminds her of the incident and claims that she "cannot remember" it, even when he describes it in detail (8:428–9)—a rather strange prelude to her display of intuitive sensitivity during his second proposal (8:436–7). See also R. F. Christian, "The Passage of Time in *Anna Karenina*," *Slavonic and East European Review*, January 1967, pp. 207–210.

11. The Maudes, pp. 37, 366; Carmichael, pp. 42, 430; Magarshack, pp. 56, 408; Garnett, pp. 45, 446.

12. This reference to Anna's "framed" beauty is echoed when she goes to the theater (9:122, 126), and it becomes reified as Levin observes Anna's portrait just before meeting her (9:285).

13. See Tolstoy, 9:27; her name is given on 9:143 and 9:147. See also 9:140.

14. The woman's "lilac" veil (seen by Seryozha) is "purple" in the Carmichael (p. 560) and the Maude (p. 476) versions.

15. Edward Wasiolek, *Tolstoy's Major Fiction* (Chicago, 1978), p. 135.

16. See Tolstoy, 8:489. The Maudes have "kicked over the traces" (pp. 271, 480)—a phrase that Carmichael (p. 318) and Magarshack (p. 306) also use but later alter to "stepping out of line" and "flung convention to the wind" (pp. 565, 530, respectively). Garnett has "flung their caps over the windmills" (p. 329) and "fling my cap over the mill" (p. 585).

5

On Levin as a Pivotal Figure

Tolstoy's creative works characteristically contain a semi-auto-biographical figure, and his two greatest novels are no exception. This figure reflects the evolution of the author's attitudes and ideas, and part of what happens is seen through his eyes. Even aside from Tolstoy's occasional didactic intrusions, we have the feeling that the author is at once outside and inside his fiction.

Critics have noted numerous differences between *War and Peace* and *Anna Karenina*, resulting from diverse conceptual intentions and, presumably, from changes in the author himself as well. Yet perhaps because the two novels are so very different, parallels between Pierre and Levin tend to pass by unnoticed. However, their creator was still grappling with many of the same problems, as these two fictional characters suggest. Moreover, Tolstoy was revising *War and Peace* for a new edition at the time he wrote *Anna Karenina* in draft form.[1] It thus seems understandable that Pierre Bezukhov sometimes seems to cast his shadow forward upon Konstantin Levin.

Both Pierre and Levin are what could be termed "dangerously natural" in social situations. When we first see them, both fail to fit in: Pierre at Anna Pavlovna's soirée, Levin at Stiva's office. It first appears that the women they eventually marry (Natasha, Kitty) will marry someone else (Andrew, Vronsky), and this promotes a parallel contrast. Pierre and Levin are strong, unhandsome, slightly clumsy, unsophisticated civilians; Andrew and Vronsky are dark and dapper, both described as brunets of medium height in uniform (5:208, 8:61).

While revealing to Vronsky Levin's hopes concerning Kitty, Stiva Oblonsky declares that Levin has "a heart of gold" (8:71). Bringing Pierre to Natasha, Andrew tells her to rely on him alone: Pierre has "a heart of gold" (5:239). These parallel descriptions of Levin and Pierre occur in contexts featuring all three members of the analogous love triangles.

Pierre and Levin are both quick to perceive that Natasha and Kitty initially favor Andrew and Vronsky. "Something very important is happening between them," Pierre thinks at the Bergs' party (5:225). And when Vronsky enters the room, Levin perceives Kitty's love by the expression on her face, "just as surely as if she had said it to him in words" (8:60). Yet both are remarkably generous. Levin seeks and finds only the best qualities in his rival (8:61); Pierre enthusiastically urges Andrew to marry Natasha (5:230). Both, moreover, reticently withdraw. In fact, Stiva Oblonsky reproaches Levin for doing so (8:191), and Pierre "avoids" Natasha, aware of "a stronger feeling for her" than a married man should have for his friend's fiancée (5:374). Yet Pierre soon concludes that the comet of 1812 "answers" the love in his soul that he feels for Natasha (5:388); Levin concludes, deeply moved by the "mysterious" change in a beautiful cloud formation, that Kitty is the one he loves (8:306). Both loves seem "cosmically confirmed."

As I have observed elsewhere, Pierre and Natasha, like Levin and Kitty, are associated by suggestions of childhood and fairy-tale-like pleasure long before they are in fact united.[2] Early in *War and Peace*, Pierre is likened to "a child in a toyshop" (4:16); early in *Anna Karenina*, Levin is compared to a "boy," a "twelve-year-old girl," and a "child" (8:27, 28, 43). Kitty's smile carries Levin off to "an enchanted world," likened to "childhood," and he associates her with an English fairy tale (8:38, 39). Natasha hides in the conservatory "as if under a cap of invisibility," a Russian fairy tale image, and Pierre pretends to be Napoleon, piercing an "invisible" enemy with his sword (4:57, 69). These descriptions tend to connect both pairs when their unions still seem quite unlikely. However, both are predicted by what I have termed Tolstoyan "unlikely prophets" (Sonya and Dolly); and with both couples, an emphasis upon "joy, fear" and the feeling that "this cannot be" precedes a happy marriage.[3]

Both happy endings are threatened by the Tolstoyan peril of flirtatious beauty. Early in *War and Peace*, Hélène displays her "victoriously acting" (*pobeditel'no dejstvuyushchuyu*) beauty, and Pierre looks at her with "almost frightened eyes" (4:18, 22). As Levin first meets Anna, she looks at him "victoriously" (*pobeditel'no*) and tenderly, which "disturbs" him (9:285). There is something almost predatory in the way Hélène intercepts Pierre's lips "with a rapid and coarse movement of her head" (4:270) as she maneuvers him into proposing. Anna, we are told, "had involuntarily done everything possible all evening to awaken love in Levin towards herself" (9:294).

The questions of "life and death" that haunt Pierre and Levin are remarkably similar. With a painful intensity well known to their creator, both desperately seek meaning in their lives. Pierre looks at the people around him, unable to understand "how they all could live without having solved the questions that occupied him" (5:70) For his part, Levin is utterly amazed at the tranquility of others; he even suspects that they may have secretly found answers to the questions that torture him (9:384). Levin, however, seems more grimly desperate. Tolstoy likens him to "a person seeking food in toyshops or gunshops," whereas Pierre was likened to "a child in a toyshop" because of his awkwardness at Anna Pavlovna's soirée (4:16).

Late in *War and Peace*, Pierre has a vision-like dream of a "globe of drops."

"In the center is God, and each drop tries to expand in order to reflect Him as widely as possible. It grows, merges, shrinks, is destroyed on the surface, sinks to the depths, and again floats forth. Here now it is Karataev who has spread out and disappeared." (7:170)

Late in *Anna Karenina*, Levin describes a similar phenomenon:

"In endless time, endless matter, and endless space, a little bubble-organism separates itself. The bubble lasts for a while, and then bursts; that bubble is—I." (9:386)

Pierre associates his "globe of drops" with the death of Platon Karataev. Platon is the Russian form of Plato; Levin, close to suicide following the parallel passage above, is beneficially inspired by a peasant named Platon who "lives for his soul and remembers God" (9:392). Pierre had been deeply moved by Platon Karataev's story of the merchant who was "forgiven" by his return, at death, to the source of divine love.

When Platon Karataev dies, a dog begins to howl where Platon had been sitting, and Pierre wonders "what it is howling about" (7:169). Sydney Schultze has noted that in the final version of *Anna Karenina*, Tolstoy cut a long passage in which Levin is terrified by a dog, which he later links in his mind with a peasant and death.[4] Tolstoy may have decided to avoid the similarity; in a draft version of *Anna Karenina*, Anna was first pictured, like Hélène in *War and Peace*, at a soirée in a low-cut dress.

Pierre and Levin are further linked with each other, and perhaps with Tolstoy himself, by repeated associations with bears. Early in *War and Peace*, Prince Vasily refers to Pierre as "this bear" (4:22), and prior to his duel with Pierre, Dolokhov suggests that Pierre is a "bear" to be hunted (5:28). Pierre himself dances with a bear and suggests taking the bear along for the evening (4:47), after which we learn that he was involved in tying a bear and a policeman back to back (4:50). In *Anna Karenina*, Levin likes to hunt and kill bears. He thinks of Kitty as "Tiny Bear," comprising, with her two sisters, the "three bears" of the English fairy tale (8:39)—perhaps a play on the fact that Tolstoy himself married one of the three Behrs sisters. Just before Levin successfully proposes to Kitty, she mentions a bear he has killed and asks him if he has any bears on his lands (8:422). In December of 1858, Tolstoy himself had killed a bear while bear-hunting; the next day another bear attacked him, biting him twice near one eye before he could escape.[5]

Levin and Pierre may thus be considered two husky, somewhat clumsy, bear-like versions of the author himself, differences between the three of them notwithstanding. Indeed, Tolstoy himself can be seen as an evolving figure that spans these quite autobiographical characters. In this sense, even their names are appropriate: "Pierre," as an awkward bear in Frenchified society, can be related to Tolstoy's early awareness that he was not "comme il faut"; "Levin" (*Lev* means lion in Russian) suggests a more mature Lev Nikolaevich Tolstoy.

Vronsky is not bear-like, and he can be considered the opposite of Levin: handsome, dapper, and socially at ease. The contrast even seems underscored because Kitty has to choose between the two men, and because her parents take opposite sides in the matter. Nevertheless, a rather strange parallel is completed, late in the novel, when Kitty declares that Anna has "enchanted" Levin—an echo of the "satanic" charm that Kitty had detected in Anna at the ball when she captivated Vronsky. As for Anna, she is said to have discerned in both Vronsky and in Levin "the common trait which had caused Kitty to fall in love with both of them" (9:294).

What is this common trait? Tolstoy does not explain, but he provides a suggestive connection: Levin and Vronsky are linked in the novel by mentions of electricity, as Schultze has observed.[6] Electricity is a topic of discussion at the party where Levin and Vronsky meet, and later, the mere mention of electricity causes Levin to ask about Vronsky (8:191). More-over, Vronsky is moved to attempt suicide by something in him likened to "a very strong charge of electricity" (8:456); Levin is saved from suicide by an action in his soul likened to that of "an electric spark" (9:393). A mysterious force thus seems to connect the two men, acting variously upon them.

Levin and Anna are kept separate for much of the novel, but when they finally meet, a force of sexual magnetism seems to draw him to her, as Kitty is quick to suspect. Long before this, however, Tolstoy had subtly associated Levin with Anna in various ways. To begin with, both are similarly introduced to us after their parallel arrivals in Moscow. Levin is simply "someone" who enters Stiva's office building (8:23); Anna is simply "a lady" who gets off the train (8:72). In both cases, the unknown person's name is given only a full page later.

At first, the Oblonsky children are very fond of Anna (8:83–4); as she falls in love with Vronsky, however, they seem to sense a change in her for the worse (8:111). These children are also initially drawn to Levin (8:295). But when, as Dolly puts it, "pride" prevents him from continuing to court Kitty, Levin himself detects a change for the worse in the Oblonsky children (8:299).

Anna and Levin both have a feeling of "splitting in two." In Anna's case, however, it suggests the conflict between her affair and her marriage (8:318, 320); with Levin, it results from his realization, after marrying Kitty, that she and he are one: ". . . now he could not tell where she ended and he began. He understood this by the agonizing feeling of division into two which he experienced at that moment." (9:55)

Levin and Anna both insistently doubt that they are loved. Just before his wedding, Levin urges Kitty to reconsider, concluding: "You cannot love me." (9:16) "If only you loved me," Anna repeatedly tells Vronsky (9:130). However, Levin's humble devotion (he insists that he is not "worthy" of Kitty) revealingly contrasts with Anna's jealousy and self-absorption as Vronsky treats her more and more coldly. The parallel flirtations of Vasenka Veslovsky lead to a similar differentiation. When Levin becomes rudely jealous of Veslovsky, Kitty tells him that he is exaggerating, "in the depths of her soul rejoicing at the force of love for her that was now expressed in his jealousy" (9:156). Dolly Oblonsky observes that Anna reluctantly but "involuntarily" flirts with Veslovsky (9:218); when Dolly reproaches Anna, she replies that it "tickles" Vronsky "and nothing more"

(9:226). "Tickling" suggests stimulation on the surface, whereas Kitty feels "in the depths of her soul" the force of Levin's love.

As Anna's attraction to Vronsky strengthens, she returns to find that her husband, son, and friend Lydia are all less attractive than she had pictured them (8:118, 122, 123). When Kitty accepts Levin's proposal, he sees all the people around him as "good, kind, and grand" (8:439, 440). After Anna's affair has begun, she is grimly said to have "died" (9:88); about to be married, Levin is jokingly termed "dead" and "departed" (9:13).

Deeply involved in her affair, Anna is likened to a drowning person who has shaken off another one (9:35). As Levin adjusts to married life, he is likened to a boatman with various problems (9:53). The proximity of these two descriptions of "floundering in water" causes us to realize that Levin's achieving equilibrium does not depend on abandoning a perishing person. In another contrasting parallel, Vronsky urges Anna not to go to the theater (9:123); Kitty urges Levin to go out to a concert (9:261). Both instances reflect the quality of the love relationship.

After his marriage, Levin wonders how he can have "such happiness" (9:59). "It's unnatural," he adds. Anna tells Dolly that she is "unforgivably happy" with Vronsky (9:198). However, Dolly perceives that Anna is not really happy after all, whereas Kitty replies to Levin that for her, "the better it is, the more natural it is."

In accumulation, these contrasts within parallels clearly imply a moral judgment in favor of Levin. Yet the parallels themselves serve to reinforce the fact that Levin and Anna resemble each other in several ways: both are vibrantly alive, outspokenly honest, strongly sensual, and heedlessly, even defiantly unconventional—sharing these qualities with the author himself. We may therefore detect an autobiographical basis for the parallel connections between Levin and Anna, as was the case with Levin and Pierre. In result of this dual association, as well as his suggested affinity with Vronsky, Levin may be seen as the pivotal figure in Tolstoy's two greatest novels.

Notes

1. See R. F. Christian, ed., *Tolstoy's Letters* (New York, 1978), 1:258. See also 1:261, 263, 265.

2. See my *Leo Tolstoy* (Boston, 1986), pp. 44, 73.

3. See my *Nabokov & Others: Patterns in Russian Literature* (Ann Arbor, 1979), pp. 47, 48, 56–7.

4. Sydney Schultze, *The Structure of Anna Karenina* (Ann Arbor, 1982), p. 168.

5. See Christian, *Tolstoy's Letters*, 1:123.

6. Schultze, p. 111.

6

Some Plays of Meaning in *Anna Karenina*

Tolstoy is justly considered a storyteller as opposed to a stylist—a "what" rather than a "how" writer—and though he was fond of puns,[1] this fondness is not reflected in most of his works. In *Anna Karenina*, however, Tolstoy indulged himself considerably, playing upon the characters' names and other words as well. We shall examine some examples of this indulgence, and speculate about its artistic effect.

Stiva Oblonsky is fond of wordplay. Early in the novel, he puns about a German clockmaker, "established" (*zavedyon*) for life "to wind up" (*zavodit'*) clocks (8:20). He also puns (9:27) on the word for "divorce" (*razvod*), which resembles the verb "to dissolve" (*razvodit'*). This reminds us of his own strained marriage and perhaps of Anna's as well. (The lawyer whom Karenin consults about a divorce is said to be "spruce as a bridegroom," 8:402.) Stiva's pun about waiting for a Jew (9:314) has been rendered by Sydney Schultze as "I had business with a Jew, and I jewst had to wait."[2] Prior to her suicide (9:355), Anna puns on the French name *Tyutkin* and the Russian *Tiutka* ("puppy; young pup, young person").[3]

Several names in the novel suggest plays of meaning, particularly in certain contexts. Perhaps most obviously, the Countess Myagkaya's name means "soft, mild, gentle"—and she is given to harsh, cutting remarks, for instance "Keep your trap shut!" (8:152) After this one, she dubs Karenin "simply stupid." Tolstoy even puns further on her name while describing Princess Betsy's husband: "Inaudibly, across the soft [*myagkomu*] carpet, he approached Countess Maygkaya." (8:150) This effect can be related to what Schultze has called "sound play with proper names" in the novel.[4]

Katavasov (whose name suggests *katavasiya*, "confusion, muddle") is a Professor of Natural Science. He has a "loud, clamorous voice" (9:269) and stretches out his words when lecturing (9:13).

Nevedomsky (whose name suggests *ne vedat'*, "not knowing") is said to be "remarkably intelligent" (9:234).

It is almost literally painful for Levin to visit the Countess Bol' in Moscow (9:262, 275), and her name means "pain" in Russian.

When Anna returns to see Seryozha on his birthday, she pretends that she is bringing a present from "Prince Skorodumov" (9:112). This name signifies "fast thoughts," and Anna must think fast to get past the servants.

Kitty, Levin's idealized sweetheart, has the surname Shcherbatskaya, which means "dented, chipped, pock-marked, gap-toothed." It can be related to the novel's motif of baring and pulling teeth, as Schultze has done with Count Bezzubov ("without teeth").[5]

As I have shown elsewhere, Tolstoy used the unlikely motif of hats to establish some ominous connections in *Anna Karenina*.[6] Some of these involve puns. At the spa, Varenka is introduced as "the one in the hat like a mushroom" (8:241). Much later, her hopes for marriage are shattered when she speaks of mushrooms "against her will." This upsets Koznyshev, who still plans to propose but then "unexpectedly" questions Varenka about mushrooms and never proposes. Her reply is literally: "In the cap there is no difference, but in the stem." It begins, in the Russian, *V shlyapke* (9:146), and her introduction was *v shlyape gribom* (8:241)—"in the hat like a mushroom."

Shortly before the scene with Koznyshev, there is much ado about making "preserves" (*varen'e*)—a word that closely resembles the name *Varen'ka* and suggests "something boiled." At one point, Tolstoy tells us that "the preserves were boiling"(*varilos' varen'e*, 9:134). Kitty then asks Levin if he knows what she and others have been discussing. "Preserves?" he asks. "Yes," she replies. "Preserves, but also how people propose." Koznyshev, she explains, may soon propose to Varenka (9:139). Tolstoy's punning thus suggests that Varenka's marriage was "brewing," although, as we have seen, the mushrooms intervened.

Another hat pun involves Princess Betsy, who wears "a hat which was soaring somewhere above her head like a mantle above a lamp" (8:463). The word *kolpachok* means a (gas) mantle, but it is also the diminutive of *kolpak*, "cap." Especially since Betsy herself is having an affair, her "soaring" hat may be associated with the idiom about "throwing bonnets beyond windmills" that she twice uses in connection with Anna's affair.[7]

When Anna and Vronsky are attracted to each other at the train station, we are told that the station-master ran past wearing ". . . a hat of an unusual color. Clearly, something unusual had happened." (8:75) The word "unusual" is *neobyknovennyj* both times, and the "something unusual" is the watchman's ominous death.

Tolstoy refers to Anna herself in three different ways, each of which can have a quite different effect. The simple form "Anna" has suggestions of informality and familiarity. "Anna Arkad'evna"—in part because "Arkadia" has, ironically, overtones of innocent pastoral happiness—reminds us that she is the sister of "Stepan Arkad'ich," whose extramarital affair receives the novel's opening focus. "Karenina" is the feminine form of Karenin, and it is also the (masculine) possessive form of his name. Early in the novel, when Anna and Vronsky are attracted to each other at the train station, she is termed "Karenina" nine times. This results in a pervasive, subtle tension between Anna's conduct and her married status. For example, she is termed "Karenina" as: "a smile lit up her face, a tender smile that related to him" (8:74). This suggests, as Tolstoy immediately declares, that she is throwing "a ball of coquetry" to Vronsky. And at the end of Part One, when Vronsky makes plans about where he can meet "Karenina," the effect is quite untranslatable into English.

Throughout much of the novel, the name Karenin, based upon the Greek *karenon* ("reason, head, intellect"), subtly reinforces Karenin's judgmental attitude towards Anna. (Somewhat similarly, in *The Death of Ivan Ilych*, the hero's surname Golovin—*golova* signifies "head" in Russian—suggests that he has functioned from the head rather than from the heart.)

"Reason" (*razum*) in *Anna Karenina* is persistently considered a potentially lethal gift to human beings. Anna tells Dolly that "reason has been given" her to prevent bringing children into the world (9:225). Prior to her suicide, Anna hears the statement that "reason is given" us to get rid of our troubles. She agrees, concluding that she ought to kill herself (9:362). The statement is said to be "in French," but Tolstoy renders "reason is given" as *dan razum* in both passages. As Levin emerges from *his* suicidal desperation, he decides that "reason" (*razum*) cannot reveal to us how to love other people (9:396). There are several such references, and the novel ends with Levin's concluding that it was impossible to find faith "by reason" (*razumom*).

Just before Vronsky's suicide attempt, he repeats to himself the single word *Razumeetsya* ("Of course"—but more literally, "It stands to reason"). This "convincing to him *razumeetsya*," Tolstoy explains, was the result of his considering, over and over, the impossible nature of his present situation and the "senselessness" of all that was left for him in life (8:457–8). Standard translations render these repetitions of *razumeetsya* "of course."[8] Prior to killing herself, Anna thinks: *"Razumeetsya, byla i lyubov' . . ."* (9:358) to express the idea that "Yes, there was love," adding however that it was mostly "pride of success." In a passage omitted in some English translations,[9] Levin connects his suicidal despair resulting from "reason" (*razum*) to a "pride of mind" (9:396).

Prior to her suicide, Anna is haunted by the fear that Vronsky will marry Princess Sorokina (9:333, 336–7, 342, 347, 356, 358, 362). *Soroka* means "magpie," and Kitty's father had earlier termed Vronsky a "quail" (*perepel*, 8:66). The name Vronsky itself can be related to *voron* ("raven") or *vorona* ("crow"), especially because of Vronsky's close-cropped black hair. Kitty's father added that Vronsky was a *shchelkopyor* ("hack" or "scribbler," suggesting "quill-snapper").

Another bird can be detected in the name Sviyazhsky (*sviyaz'* means a "wigeon"); and of Chirikov, Levin's best man (whose name can be related to *chirikat'*, "to chirp, to twitter"), we are told that he "gaily and good-naturedly kept up any conversation" (9:13). However, Chirikov may also suggest *chiriki* ("shoes"), especially since the name of Vronsky's friend Golenishchev comes from *golenishche* ("the top of a boot").

Vasenka Veslovsky's name aptly suggests *vesyolost'* ("gaiety, merry-making"); it also contrasts ironically with the painful jealousy he arouses in Levin. And, given Veslovsky's penchant for flirting, Tolstoy may also have punned in having him introduced as a "passionate hunter" (9:150). As I have shown, Kitty's passion for Vronsky is indirectly likened to "scarlet fever" elsewhere in the novel.[10]

Even the two country estates, didactically contrasted during Veslovsky's and Dolly's visits, have names with potential plays of meaning. Pokrovskoe, Levin's estate, suggests a protective cover (*pokrov*) or haven. At Vozdvizhenskoe, Vronsky's estate, derived from *vozdvigat'* ("to raise, erect"), the hospital construction is said to be progressing rapidly (9:209). This progress, of course, ironically contrasts with the concurrent deterioration of Anna's and Vronsky's relationship.

What, we may ask, is the artistic effect of these various plays of meaning throughout *Anna Karenina?* First, they add a dimension of subtle pleasure as we encounter them. Moreover, some of them tend to suggest that Fate is playing a cat-and-mouse game with the characters, set as they are in a world of exacting social conduct and flexible moral standards. Particularly in connection with Kitty's scarlet-fever-related passion, Anna's ultimately fatal affair, the train watchman's death, and Koznyshev's mushroom-stifled proposal, Tolstoy's playfulness adds a cynical, fateful note. Yet perhaps because of the author's deeply-felt, earnest moral position, this playfulness tends to escape our notice. As is well known, Tolstoy expressed great dissatisfaction both with the subject matter of his novel (adultery) and with its execution. The novel was not even well done, he insisted. Quite possibly, a contributing factor in this condemnation was Tolstoy's developing conviction—later expressed in *What is Art?*—that art is emphatically not pleasure, an intricate puzzle, or a game.

Notes

1. As Sydney Schultze has noted, Gol'denveizer reports that Tolstoy was fond of jokes featuring puns, and Andrei Biely has a Karenin-like character who tells similar jokes in *Peterburg*. See Sydney Schultze, *The Structure of Anna Karenina* (Ann Arbor, 1982), p. 166.

2. Schultze, p. 75.

3. *Ibid.*, p. 166. See also Tolstoy, 8:66.

4. Schultze, p. 75.

5. *Ibid.*, pp. 113–4.

6. See my *Leo Tolstoy* (Boston, 1986), p. 86.

7. See Chapter Four, above.

8. Louise and Aylmer Maude (New York, 1970), p. 380; David Magarshack (New York, 1961), p. 423; Joel Carmichael (New York, 1978), p. 446; Constance G. Garnett (New York, 1966), pp. 462–3.

9. Magarshack has this passage, but the Maudes, Carmichael, and Garnett omit it. When Tolstoy has Levin *refer back to* the passage (9:408), the Maude translation is more accurate, but Carmichael and Garnett render the reference less puzzling.

10. See my *Nabokov & Others: Patterns in Russian Literature* (Ann Arbor, 1979), p. 49.

7

Dostoevsky's Anticipatory Style

The vivid impact of Dostoevsky's writing derives in part from carefully prepared climactic situations and episodes. A characteristic technique is to create anticipatory suggestions that linger in the reader's mind. These suggestions are often imagined, dreamed, or remembered. They then vividly materialize in the anticipated circumstance or event.

As *The Double* begins, Mr. Golyadkin consults a mirror. At first, he is "entirely satisfied" with his image (1:210), but this soon gives way to forebodings of an alien pimple jumping up—and of some impending failure. All this anticipates Mr. Golyadkin's perceptions of his double, whom he repeatedly takes for his image in a mirror (263, 299, 357). His initial satisfaction, moreover, soon gives way to horror at the double's treacheries. Even the hypothetical pimple that might "jump up" can be seen to materialize as the upstart double himself.

In *The Insulted and The Injured*, Prince Valkovski says that he is fond of winning someone's friendship and then "showing him his tongue" when the new friend least expects it (3:269). He then describes a lunatic in a long cloak who abruptly exposed himself to respectable people on the street. Valkovski likens the lunatic's pleasure to his own fondness for figurative tongue exposures, and at the end of their conversation, Ivan Petrovich declares that the Prince has truly resembled the lunatic in the cloak (282).

Early in *Crime and Punishment*, Raskolnikov exclaims: "God! Will I really—will I really take the axe and beat her on the head until I crush her skull . . .?" (5:65) Raskolnikov has just dreamed of a mare, brutally beaten on the head. The dream (itself a dramatized recollection) and the thought it engenders vividly materialize in the murder scene. In Philip

Rahv's words: "The dream's imagery is entirely prospective in that it points ahead, anticipating the murder Raskolnikov is plotting. . . ."[1]

The anticipatory function of the novel's opening focus is more subtle. Avoiding his landlady, to whom he owes money, Raskolnikov decides to "slink down the stairs like a cat and slip away unseen." This is echoed by his slinking down the stairs (again, "like a cat") to steal the axe (75)—and also by his suspenseful departure from the murder scene by sneaking down the stairs (92). As he does so, his feverish panic echoes the unusually strong fear of meeting his landlady that had "struck" him as the novel began (6). At that point, he had thought it strange to be "so afraid of trifles," considering the thing he "planned to do." Dostoevsky thus combined Raskolnikov's intense fear of being caught on the stairs with a vague but suggestive reference to the episode whose ending it anticipated.[2]

Raskolnikov had overheard a conversation six weeks earlier: a student jokingly declared that he could kill and rob Alyona Ivanovna without a twinge of conscience (71). Moreover, his justification of doing good deeds with the money presumably parallels the plan of the "former student" Raskolnikov: he considers it "a predestination, a sign" that the student should express *"exactly the same thoughts."*

Like Raskolnikov's dream that anticipates the murder scene, his dream that replays it contains forward-leaning details. When he awakens, this dream seems to be continuing because of the "wide-open door" (288) of his room. The fly that "buzzes" and "beats against the glass" is also a concretization, as George Steiner has noted.[3] Discussing these reified details, Richard Peace suggests that Svidrigailov "is the continuation of Raskolnikov's dream—the old woman who has come to life again."[4] As Peace explains, Svidrigailov proceeds to discuss the reappearance of the dead in the form of ghosts. Still another factor is that Svidrigailov sits down on a chair and lowers his head, assuming the position of the old woman in Raskolnikov's dream.

Raskolnikov's avowal to Porfiry Petrovich that he "literally" believes in the Resurrection of Lazarus (271) quite obviously anticipates his insistence that Sonya read the story to him later. However, as Rahv has observed, Raskolnikov himself can be considered "a kind of Lazarus whom Sonya strives to raise from the dead."[5]

Early in the novel, Raskolnikov notices a young girl in the park, apparently intoxicated and exhausted. He prevents a man from taking advantage of her, calling him "Svidrigailov" (52). He then realizes in horror that his sister Dunya could be reduced to such a state (56). Raskolnikov is of course remembering his mother's letter, but his thoughts also anticipate the climactic scene wherein Dunya almost kills the lecherous Svidrigailov. As with Raskolnikov's dream of the mare, his thoughts in the park draw upon the past but lean towards the future.

In the opening scene of *The Idiot*, the ingratiating Lebedev catches and weighs Rogozhin's every word "as if he was hunting for a diamond" (6:12). This image materializes two pages later in Rogozhin's story of the earrings he bought for Nastasia Filippovna: "each one with a diamond almost the size of a walnut" (14).[6] Prince Myshkin declares that he liked Rogozhin "especially" when he told the story "about the diamond earrings" (17)—and at the end of the novel, when Rogozhin shows Myshkin the corpse of Nastasia Filippovna, Dostoevsky describes her "diamonds, taken off and scattered on a little table," gleaming beside her body (686).

Myshkin's breaking the Chinese vase at the Epanchins' (620) is clearly anticipated—as is the fit he fears he will have there—by his conversation with Aglaya (594–5). However, there are two additional factors. First, Myshkin treats General Ivolgin as if the latter "were made of porcelain, and he was continually afraid of shattering him" (558). Second, Hippolite observes that Myshkin treats him "like a porcelain cup" (591). Richard Peace has associated Myshkin's two attitudes with his breaking the vase, noting that "there is something of the vase's fragility in human relationships."[7] William J. Leatherbarrow makes the same connection, and declares that by the end of the novel Myshkin "becomes the destroyer of form."[8] The two porcelain images endow the vase incident with a subtle sense of inevitability, especially when it strikes Myshkin as "a prophecy come true!" (620) As we have seen, Raskolnikov considered the conversation he overheard (anticipating his murder of Alyona Ivanovna) to be "a predestination, a sign."

Early in *The Idiot*, Ganya becomes so angry at Prince Myshkin that he is almost ready "to spit" (102); after this, Varya actually does spit in Ganya's face (135). Ganya also glares at Myshkin "as if he wanted to reduce him to ashes" just three pages before his ordeal with the burning packet of money (195). As with Myshkin and the broken vase, these two descriptions of Ganya add a tinge of inevitability to the episodes that follow, even if the reader does not consciously make the connections. Long before Nastasia Filippovna sets Rogozhin's money ablaze, Rogozhin declared that her beauty "burned right through" him when he first saw her (14). As the money burns, moreover, Nastasia Filippovna stands beside the fireplace, her "fiery gaze" fixed upon Ganya (199). He himself stares into the fire with an "insane smile." This, in turn, follows the revelation that Nastasia's father became insane after his wife died in a fire (46–7).

Anticipation enhances our introduction to Nastasia Filippovna. When Rogozhin tells his story of the diamond earrings, he emphasizes her striking beauty. Myshkin later beholds her "astonishing loveliness" in a photographic portrait (35). Finally, the Prince admits her to the Ivolgins' apartments and recognizes her "at once from her portrait" (117).

George Steiner has observed that the picture of Nastasia Filippovna "is one of those physical 'properties' (Muishkin's cross, Rogojin's knife) which connect the bewilderingly diverse strands of narrative and give them coherence."[9] As we shall see, Dostoevsky suggestively prepared for the principal episodes involving the cross and the knife. As with Nastasia Filippovna, moreover, pictures are involved in both cases.

At the Epanchins', Myshkin describes his idea for a painting: a condemned man about to be executed, straining to kiss the cross that a priest holds out to him. "The cross and the head—there is the picture. . . ." (76) Later, after seeing a painting depicting "the Saviour, who had just been taken down from the cross" (247), the Prince tells Rogozhin about a drunken soldier who sold him his tin cross as a silver one (249). They then exchange, at Rogozhin's suggestion, his gold cross for the tin one that Myshkin had purchased (251). Richard Peace has linked Rogozhin's desire to wear the cross of the "seller of Christ" with his attempt to murder Myshkin, which it suggestively anticipates.[10]

At the Epanchins', Myshkin establishes a major theme in the novel: the awareness of impending death. His long discussion on this topic (25–7) is followed by his vivid speculations about how a man allots his last five minutes before being executed (69–71). It is then that he describes his idea for a painting depicting a condemned man a minute before the guillotine blade falls (73–6). Later, when Rogozhin's knife is "already descending upon him" (267), Myshkin is saved by an epileptic fit, likened to a sort of writhing, screaming death.

More specifically than by the guillotine, the ultimately lethal use of Rogozhin's knife is variously anticipated throughout the novel. He suggests to Myshkin that Nastasia is marrying him "because my knife is waiting for her" (244). Others have already told her that Rogozhin may slit her throat (239)—and when Rogozhin abruptly asks Myshkin's opinion, he replies that Rogozhin may indeed do so (241–2). Before leaving, Myshkin absentmindedly fingers Rogozhin's new knife (245–6). He then recalls having seen some "merchandise" in a shop window (254)—gradually revealed to be a knife (263) that he associates with a "foreboding" (265). Edward Wasiolek has suggested that by acting to confirm Rogozhin's suspicions and by imagining what Rogozhin will do, the Prince now "anticipates"—and "in anticipating," actually "helps to create"—Rogozhin's attack upon him with the knife at the hotel.[11]

Much earlier, Myshkin's discussion of what people experience just before they are killed included those whose throats are cut by bandits while they plead for mercy or attempt to escape (26). Examining Nastasia Filippovna's portrait, the Prince speculates that Rogozhin "might marry her, but would probably slit her throat a week later" (42). She herself suggests that Ganya Ivolgin would slit a throat for money (187), adding that she has recently read about people who now slit a friend's throat "like a sheep's."

In Dostoevsky's Russian, Nastasia's saying "like a sheep's" (*kak barana*) subtly links the "throat-slitting" with her own name, Barashkova (*barashkovyj* means "lambskin"). Myshkin echoes this image when he tells Rogozhin about a man who slit his friend's throat like a sheep's and stole his watch (249), and Rogozhin soon tells the Prince that although he took his cross, he will not "slit his throat" for his "watch" (253). As Peace has observed, Rogozhin makes it clear that by the word "watch" he means Nastasia Filippovna.[12] Dostoevsky thus blended muted anticipations of Rogozhin's attempts on Myshkin's and Nastasia Filippovna's lives. Earlier, when Nastasia awarded Ganya the slightly burned money, she declared: "otherwise, he might slit my throat" (201). The anticipatory effect of these and other references to throat-slitting is diminished by English translations that render *zarezat'* as "to kill" or "to murder."

In Nastasia's last letter to Aglaya, she mentions a razor hidden in Rogozhin's drawer and again refers to her reading about slitting a friend's throat (517). Rogozhin, who reads the letter, laughs about the razor (520). Finally, not long before Rogozhin fatally stabs Nastasia Filippovna, Myshkin finds her ". . . in a state resembling total insanity: she shrieked, trembled, and cried out that Rogozhin . . . would kill her in the night . . . he'd slit her throat!" (669)

Early in *The Devils*, we learn that a gentleman named Gaganov is fond of saying: "No, sir, they won't lead me by the nose!" (7:48) Stavrogin then seizes Gaganov's nose between two fingers and leads him around the room.

Kirillov tells Stavrogin that people are unhappy because "Everything now is pain and fear." (123) "He who conquers pain and fear," he insists, "will himself be a god." Later, when Shatov strikes Stavrogin's face, the narrator suggests that in his powerful self-control, Stavrogin resembled certain legendary brave men who set as their goal "the conquest of fear" (217). Stavrogin also resembles "a man who, in order to test his fortitude, had seized a red-hot metal bar and clenched it in his hand, trying to conquer the unbearable pain for the next ten seconds, and had finally conquered it." He thus reacts to Shatov's blow with the two "conquerings" proposed by Kirillov for becoming a god.

The fortunetelling of Marya Timofeevna has a still more far-reaching anticipatory function. According to her cards, she tells Shatov, "It always comes out the same: a journey, a wicked man, someone's treachery, a death-bed, a letter from somewhere, unexpected news." (153) Late in the novel, these prophecies are fulfilled in the same sequence. The "journey" suggests the chapter entitled "The Traveler," in which Shatov's wife finally returns. The "wicked man" construes as Peter Verkhovensky, and his "treachery" is the murder of Shatov himself. The "death-bed" becomes Shatov's burial in the pond. The "letter from somewhere" is Stavrogin's letter to Dasha, which he ends by revealing his location; Dasha and Stavrogin's mother rush there to discover the "unexpected news" of his suicide.

We should note that Marya Timofeevna tells these prophecies *to* Shatov—and that the first four directly concern him. She also tells Shatov that she buried her baby "in the pond" (156). Marya's apparent aberration (Stavrogin declares that she is a virgin, and she herself admits that the baby may never have existed) thus supplements her prophecy of Shatov's own "death-bed" when he himself is buried in a pond (630).

When Stavrogin visits Marya Timofeevna, she abruptly exclaims, "I'm not afraid of your knife!" (294) This puzzles Stavrogin, and she continues: "Yes, knife! You have a knife in your pocket. You thought I was sleeping, but I saw it. When you came in a little while ago, you took out your knife!" He leaves, repeating to himself "A knife, a knife!"—and meets Fedka, who produces a real knife (295). It is presumably this knife that kills Marya Timofeevna, and in a sense it can be considered "Stavrogin's," although Dostoevsky purposely obscures the degree of Stavrogin's responsibility for her death. Shortly before Marya's declarations about the knife, she awakened, "recoiled" from Stavrogin, and "raised her arm as if in self-defense" (288). We later learn that when the knife killed her, she: "struggled with her murderer while awake" (540). The raising of her arm in self-defense apparently resulted from a "bad dream" about Stavrogin, and although she does not say what he was doing in the nightmare, this dream and her reaction combine with her defensive hallucinations about the knife to form an inferential description of her own murder—much as her prophecies and aberration about a baby combine to suggest Shatov's murder and burial.

In conversation with Kirillov, Stavrogin mentions "a person who insults and rapes a little girl," and Kirillov soon calls his attention to a spider crawling on the wall (252). In the section "At Tikhon's," originally intended to appear about two hundred pages later in the novel, Stavrogin describes how he took advantage of a young girl sexually and remained in the next room while she hanged herself. A tiny red spider repeatedly catches his attention, and he associates this spider with his peeking through a chink in the door to observe the terrible consequences of his crime.[13] Ralph Matlaw, who discusses in detail Dostoevsky's use of spider images, has made this connection.[14]

The name Karamazov suggests "punishment-stained" (*kara*, punishment; *mazat'*, to smear, daub, stain), and each of Fyodor Karamazov's three sons is seen to have some responsibility for his death. Smerdyakov, putatively his fourth son and his murderer, has a name that signifies "reeking." Early in the novel, Rakitin tells Alyosha that Father Zosima has ". . . smelled out a crime. It reeks [*smerdit*] at your house." (9:101)[15] In context, this explains why Zosima bowed down to Dmitri, who, he sensed, was to have a great future ordeal. A large part of the ordeal is being found guilty of the "reeking one's" crime.

Captain Snegiryov excuses the bad odor in his dwelling by saying that "dead people smell even worse." (9:254) He tells this *to* Alyosha, who will later be so dismayed by the odor of Father Zosima's corpse (407). The effect thus resembles that of Marya Timofeevna's statements *to* Shatov.

Also prior to Father Zosima's death, Father Ferapont claims that he once killed a devil, which probably rotted in the corner, reeking, although people could not see or smell it (212). As in Rakitin's declaration, "reeking" is *smerdit*. Father Ferapont also claims that before killing the devil, he crushed its tail in "the crack of the door." Much later, in a chapter entitled "The Little Devil," Lisa purposely crushes her finger in the crack of the door (10:98). In its immediate context, the incident is anticipated by Alyosha's reference to "the need to crush something good" (93) and by Lisa's story of the boy whose fingers were cut off from both hands (95).

Early in the novel, Ivan Karamazov declares to his father that there is no God: it is merely the devil, mocking people (9:171). He then admits that there is no devil, either. These views anticipate the mocking devil that Ivan believes he sees (and converses with) after his father's death. Towards the end of their conversation, the devil tells Ivan of a man who committed suicide (10:175); they are soon interrupted by Alyosha, who reports that "Smerdyakov shot himself an hour ago." The man in the devil's story had evidently lost his faith during confession with a holy father who disillusioned him; Smerdyakov had lost his faith while confessing his crime and becoming disillusioned in Ivan.

Indeed, Smerdyakov assumed that Ivan had subtly instructed him to murder Fyodor Pavlovich and had even condoned the deed. Hence, Smerdyakov's claim that he was merely the instrument employed by the "legitimate killer" Ivan (10:150). Earlier, a peasant had killed a goose, inspired by Kolya Krasotkin's idea of pushing a cart so that it rolled over the goose's neck. Kolya, accused of putting the peasant up to it, coolly insisted that he "merely expressed the basic idea and spoke only of its being feasible" (10:52). Although Kolya had planned to manipulate the goose, it obligingly stretched out its neck before the wheel of the cart; "grinning wickedly," Ivan observed to his (about to be murdered) father that he himself was sending him away to Chermashnya (9:350). Ralph Matlaw has observed that the goose episode "also points ahead to the trial, for the amused judge condemns the peasant (the instrument) to pay, while he dismisses Kolja (the instigator) with a warning to stop projecting such schemes."[16]

At the end of Ivan's Grand Inquisitor Legend, Christ, instead of answering the Inquisitor's reproachful interrogations, ". . . quietly goes over to the old man and gently kisses him on his bloodless ninety-year-old lips." (9:330) Ivan then declares that he will not renounce his theory that "all is permitted" and asks Alyosha if he will therefore renounce him: "Alyosha got up, walked over to him, and quietly kissed him on the lips." (331) As with many Dostoevskian anticipations, Alyosha's action draws upon the emotional atmosphere of its counterpart and thus rings particularly true in context.

Despite his persistent disparagements of Dostoevsky, Vladimir

Nabokov has given him due credit for "whetting the reader's attention" and "prolonging the suspense."[17] Vyacheslav Ivanov has provided an insight into this process:

> In the circumstantial and seemingly exaggerated matter-of-factness of Dostoevsky's style no detail however small may be omitted: so closely do all particulars of the action cohere to the unity of the successive episodes of the story—separated though these are by numerous discursive passages.[18]

As we have seen, these successive episodes are often concretizations of earlier hints, suggestions, and images. Thus anticipated, the episodes seem particularly vivid; they have a cumulative impact upon the reader. They also seem surprisingly convincing: the most bizarre, startling situations seem somehow forseeable and/or faintly familiar. The range is vast—from Mr. Golyadkin's prophetic confrontation with his mirror to the reflection of Christ's kiss in Alyosha's answer to Ivan. It includes dreams, forebodings, recounted stories, and even descriptive phrases in the narration ("as if looking for a diamond," "reduce him to ashes") or remarks by the characters themselves ("they won't lead me by the nose," "it reeks at your house"). In the most dramatic instances, the author's creation of anticipatory suggestions can be likened to the lighting of a fuse (Raskolnikov's question about the axe; various references to Rogozhin's knife). Dostoevsky, we could say, anticipates a scene or episode until it explosively occurs.

Notes

1. Philip Rahv, "Dostoevsky in *Crime and Punishment*," in: Rene Wellek, ed., *Dostoevsky: A Collection of Critical Essays* (Englewood Cliffs, N.J., 1962), p. 18.

2. Richard Peace considers Raskolnikov's landlady "linked with Alyona on the very first page of the novel," adding that his being summoned to the police station (to pay a debt) immediately after the murder—at Alyona's instigation—"appears almost as some sort of retribution from the grave." (*Dostoevsky: An Examination of The Major Novels*, Cambridge, 1975, pp. 35, 40.)

3. George Steiner, *Tolstoy or Dostoevsky: An Essay in the Old Criticism* (New York, 1961), p. 143. Ralph Matlaw has associated this fly with Raskolnikov's earlier attempt to assure himself that he was unobserved: "A fly flew by and saw it. Is it possible?" See Ralph E. Matlaw, "Recurrent Imagery in Dostoevskij," *Harvard Slavic Studies*, No. 3 (1957), p. 211.

4. Peace, p. 42.

5. Rahv, p. 22.

6. A similar effect occurs late in the novel when Aglaya declares that other people are not even worthy of picking up Prince Myshkin's "handkerchief" (387). She then admits that she herself will never marry Myshkin—and covers her face with her own handkerchief (388).

7. Peace, p. 115.

8. William J. Leatherbarrow, *Fedor Dostoevsky* (Boston, 1981), p. 114.

9. Steiner, p. 155.

10. Peace, p. 91.

11. Edward Wasiolek, *Dostoevsky: The Major Fiction* (Cambridge, 1964), pp. 105–6.

12. Peace, p. 91. See also p. 119.

13. See F. M. Dostoevskij, *U Tikhona* (New York, 1964), pp. 57, 58.

14. Matlaw, pp. 217–8.

15. Peace has made this connection, p. 225.

16. Ralph E. Matlaw, *The Brothers Karamazov: Novelistic Technique* (The Hague, 1957), p. 26.

17. Vladimir Nabokov, *Lectures on Russian Literature*, ed. Fredson Bowers (New York, 1981), pp. 132, 128.

18. Vyacheslav Ivanov, *Freedom and The Tragic Life: A Study in Dostoevsky*, Trans. Norman Cameron (New York, 1960), p. 10.

8

Dostoevskian Staircase Drama

Vyacheslav Ivanov and George Steiner have both suggested that Dostoevsky's works resemble plays in many respects.[1] Steiner, who quotes Thomas Mann's opinion that Dostoevsky's novels are "colossal dramas," declares: "Dostoevsky is an example of a novelist who must be read with a constant commitment of our visual imagination."[2] Some of Dostoevsky's most dramatic moments are graphically staged on staircases; we shall trace the development of this phenomenon and examine its artistic function.

P. M. Bitsilli has observed that in Dostoevsky's works: "Exceedingly often, the most terrifying scenes are played out on staircases." Bitsilli notes that Dostoevskian stairways are typically narrow, dirty, dark, and winding. It is easy "to slip and fall downwards" on them, as well as to hide from—and to lie in wait for—others. In the examples he gives, people constantly pursue others, often overtaking them in dramatic confrontations. Bitsilli notes that the function of staircases in the works of the French writer Julien Green is remarkably similar to their role in Dostoevsky. In *The Brothers Karamazov*, Dostoevsky has Madame Khokhlakova rush to meet Alyosha on the stairs, remarking that they now resemble characters in Griboedov's play *Woe From Wit*, where "everything fateful happened on the stairs." (9:278). Although Bitsilli refrains from claiming influence (as do I), we have here the curious, remote possibility of Green's being indebted to Griboedov via Dostoevsky. Bitsilli concludes that "the image of stairs" in Dostoevsky serves as "a symbol of the agonizing and 'heavy' psychical processes of all his heroes, and it is closely connected with . . . the doubles whom they fear and yet towards whom they are attracted with insurmountable force."[3] This may be overstated, but it aptly emphasizes the "psychical" intensity associated with the Dostoevskian staircase "image."

Dostoevskian staircase drama begins in *Poor People*, when Varvara Alekseyevna writes to Makar Devushkin: "I can't even walk down our stairs: everyone looks at me, points a finger at me, and says such dreadful things; yes, they bluntly say that *I have taken up with a drunkard.*" (1:170)

In *The Double*, the theme is already quite fully developed. First, Mr. Golyadkin runs "down the stairs with a slight palpitation in his heart" (1:213) and drives to his doctor's. Climbing the stairs, he tries to catch his breath and restrain "the pounding of his heart, which had the habit of pounding on all other people's staircases" (215). Deciding that it would be "stupid to hide," Mr. Golyadkin continues up the stairs and prepares to ring the bell, decides that it might be better to return tomorrow, and—suddenly hearing someone's footsteps on the stairs—rings with great determination. This episode contains several characteristic details of Dostoevskian staircase drama: losing one's breath, having heart palpitations, a reference to hiding, and hearing suspenseful footsteps or voices. Others are: pursuit, evasion by slipping past someone, falling, eyes that flash in the darkness, and the sound of a door slamming. In context, these details often help to point up a character's thoughts and feelings. Here, Dostoevsky vividly hints at Mr. Golyadkin's precarious grip on reality, his paranoid fears, and his masochistic ambivalence even with regard to seeking help.

Soon Mr. Golyadkin is refused admission to the Berendeyevs'. Andrey Filippovich stands above him on the stairs, "looking as if he was ready to jump directly into his eyes" (233–4). Voicing incoherent objections "from below," Mr. Golyadkin mounts one step after another until Andrey Filippovich, retreating upwards, "jumps" inside, "slamming the door behind him." Painfully confused, Mr. Golyadkin hears "voices and steps coming up the stairs from below." Pulling up his collar, he weakly stumbles down the stairs, stepping off into the mud without even waiting for his carriage.

The positions and motions in this episode are vividly staged. The slamming door points up the hero's painful isolation, while his weak, stumbling descent suggests his (quite literal) debasement. Not only does he step down into the mud, Mr. Golyadkin then desires inwardly "to sink beneath the ground or to hide in a mousehole." Such is the momentum of his degradation.

After this, Mr. Golyadkin waits for "over two hours" on the Berendeyevs' cold back stairs,[4] looking in at Klara Olsufyevna's birthday celebration (239). In several later works, Dostoevsky had his characters wait on staircases in awkward isolation for long periods of time.[5] Here, Mr. Golyadkin's plight on the stairs spans four pages until he invades the party and is ejected. Finding himself on the dark stairs, he stumbles downwards, feeling "as if he were falling into an abyss" (248).

Mr. Golyadkin soon follows a "stranger" to his own apartment: "The stairs were dark, damp, and dirty." (256) They are so heaped with rubbish that a nocturnal visitor might have "to traverse them for half an hour, in danger of breaking his legs." But the stranger seems to know his way. As Mr. Golyadkin rushes up behind him, the bottom of the stranger's overcoat strikes him "two or three times" on the nose—a vividly staged humiliation. This scene is echoed when Mr. Golyadkin chases his double up the stairs to his office feeling "a strong palpitation of his heart and a shiver in all his limbs" (326), whereupon the double viciously insults him before his colleagues. Still later, at his Excellency's, the double insults Mr. Golyadkin once again, staring down defiantly into his eyes "from the height of the stairs" (359). At the end, Mr. Golyadkin is trapped on the Berendeyevs' "brightly lit staircase" (373) with a crowd of people and his doctor. As he looks back, the "brightly lit staircase" is filled with inquisitive-eyed people including Olsufy Ivanovich, who looks down intently "from the uppermost landing of the stairs." As if caught in a spotlight himself, the deranged hero is thus observed from above with near clinical detachment as he makes his final descent.

In *Netochka Nezvanova,* Dostoevsky used staircases to focus four themes: the heroine's painful devotion to her stepfather Efimov, the budding love between the two young girls, the drama involving the complicated bulldog Sir John Falstaff, and Netochka's increasingly ominous relationship with Pyotr Aleksandrovich. With Efimov, the drama involving money is constantly played out upon the stairs (2:98, 108–9, 112–3), where the little girl waits for him, "often shaking and having turned blue from the cold" (102). It is on the stairs that Netochka first gives Katya a furtive kiss (156), and their nocturnal passion is anticipated by the fact that climbing the stairs ostensibly causes the heart of each girl (164, 165) to beat violently. It is on the stairs that Netochka discerns the "terrible revenge" that Katya is planning upon the old Countess (158), and when Katya gives Falstaff access to the forbidden staircase—which he sometimes stalks for three days at a time—the frightening bulldog triumphantly rushes upwards, baring his teeth (160). Finally, as the suspenseful relationship intensifies between Netochka and Pyotr Aleksandrovich, the mere sound of his voice on the stairs, descending from above, causes her to shudder "as if scorched" (208).

In the climactic scene of *The Village of Stepanchikovo and Its Inhabitants*, as Foma Opiskin spews out insults, Egor throws him through a glass door, causing him to fall "head over heels down the seven stone steps" leading to the yard (2:598). "Fragments of shattered glass" also fall upon the steps—a potential suggestion of Opiskin's shattered reputation.

Much of the staircase drama in *The Insulted and The Injured* features little Nelli, who eerily hides on the dark stairs after her grandfather's death (3:62–3, 182) and subsequently (241, 242, 304, 305). She later recounts how she had waited on the cold stairs for money from her grandfather, who finally struck the steps with his stick, threw her some copper coins that rolled down the stairs, cursed her mother, and slammed the door (348–9).

Several characters reveal their true feelings on stairways. Visiting Natasha, Prince Volkovski "swears like a coachman" at the "narrow, dirty, steep, never illuminated" stairs (188). Then, recognizing Vanya, the Prince abruptly appears delighted to see him. Conversing with Natasha, the Prince refers to her "repulsive staircase" (204), and she exposes his hypocrisy in so doing: by withholding money from Alyosha, he had forced her to live in a place with "this staircase" (211).

When Katya finally visits Natasha, she declares that her heart is beating strongly. Vanya attributes it to the "steep stairs" (321), and Katya agrees, but it is clear that she is apprehensive about meeting her rival. Having stopped to catch her breath, Katya continues up the stairs "decisively." Shortly thereafter, Vanya demonstrates his devotion to Natasha as he waits for "an hour and a half" on the stairs with "boundless pain" in his heart (329).

The emotional ordeal of Natasha's father is also revealed on her stairs, as Vanya watches him come agonizingly close to visiting the daughter he has disowned (317). Pretending that he was looking for someone else, the proud, stubborn old man adds, with unwitting eloquence: "I was mistaken." Only at the end of the novel, he tells Natasha how often he had climbed her stairs and waited, listening, outside her door (356).

In *Notes From The Underground*, one of the most vivid pictures with which the protagonist threatens Liza is of a drunken prostitute, locked out in the cold at nine in the morning, sitting on some "stone stairs" (4:218). Half naked, with blood flowing from her nose and teeth, she wails and bangs a dried fish "against the steps of the stairs," mocked by a crowd of cabmen and drunken soldiers. And what if she remembered, asks the Underground Man, "while banging that dirty fish against the steps," her former, pure years when she had a chance for love and happiness? Finally, when he cruelly insults Liza, and she leaves:

> "Liza! Liza!" I shouted down the stairs, but timidly, in a low voice.
> There was no answer, but I seemed to hear her footsteps on the lower stairs.
> "Liza!" I shouted more loudly.
> No answer. But at that moment I heard from below the heavy outer glass door to the street open with a creak and then slam tightly. A rumble rose up the stairs. (241)

As the slamming door dramatically suggests, the Underground Man is cut off from Liza forever. And the "rumble" (*gul*) that rises up the stairwell reflects his half-deranged awareness that he has finalized the hollowness in his life.

In *The Eternal Husband,* Dostoevsky used sound effects on stairways to increase the suspense. When Velchaninov realizes that Trusotsky is coming to see him, he listens "with all his might to the rustle of the expected footsteps on the stairs" (4:450). He even senses Trusotsky, beyond the closed door, stealthily listening on the stairs below.

While on the stairs himself, Velchaninov hears someone abusing a child who pleads for mercy—a scene he pictures in vivid detail even before meeting Liza (467–8). Finally, fearing that Trustosky will try to murder him in the dark, Velchaninov has a delirious dream about a noisy, agitated crowd on a staircase (560–1), causing his heart to beat violently. Awakening, he struggles in the darkness with Trusotsky, who cuts him with a razor.

The intensity of Dostoevskian staircase drama reached a peak in *Crime and Punishment*. Indeed, the episode in which Raskolnikov climbs the stairs to kill and rob Alyona Ivanovna and especially its companion scene, wherein he is trapped with his two victims by strangers on the stairs before he can escape, are unusually suspenseful, even for Dostoevsky. Climbing the stairs, Raskolnikov keeps listening with a desperate intensity. His pounding heart, which he pressed with one hand, beats "harder, harder, harder" (5:81). He rings, but there is no answer. Pressing his ear against the door, he seems to hear "the cautious rustle of an arm near the doorknob and something like the swish of a dress against the door." Someone, he decides, is lurking silently on the other side, "also listening intently with one ear pressed against the door." Dostoevsky thus employs the same device of blind-but-vivid mutual listening as in *The Eternal Husband*.

Attempting to leave, Raskolnikov stands on the stairs, feverishly aware of the voices and footsteps of the two men, who, it suspensefully develops, are coming up to visit the woman he has just murdered. He rushes back in and locks the door: "They now stood opposite each other, as he had done recently with the old woman, when the door separated them, and he was intently listening." (88) Terrified, Raskolnikov hears the men's evolving suspicions and their decision to fetch the janitor. He even pictures both men from their breathing and the sound of their voices. Finally, he manages to hide in a freshly painted room two flights below, while the investigators run noisily past him up the stairs.

All this is anticipated and echoed by several other stairway episodes. As the novel begins, Raskolnikov sneaks past his landlady's door on the stairs "like a cat" (6), already thinking of what he has planned to do. He then walks up Alyona Ivanovna's "dark, narrow staircase," and her sharp eyes regard him suspiciously in the darkness (8–9), as they will before he kills her. When he steals the axe, Raskolnikov is again likened to "a cat" on the stairs (75).

The murder scene is echoed by Raskolnikov's delirious dream of his landlady, who howls, moans, and groans as she is beaten on the stairs (121–3), by his cautious return up the stairs to the scene of the crime (179), and by his suspenseful dream that grotesquely replays the stair-climbing and the murder itself (287–8). The freshly painted room on Alyona's stairs is echoed by the smell of fresh paint at the police station. This smell combines with the "steep, narrow, slop-covered stairs" that he climbs there (100) to promote his dizziness and fainting spell. Dostoevsky thus uses the stairs to intensify the murderer's nauseous, vertiginous fear and guilt.

At the end of the novel, when Raskolnikov finally returns to the police station to confess: "Again the same litter, the same eggshells on the winding staircase . . . steam and stench." (551) Raskolnikov then learns of Svidrigailov's suicide, and his vertiginous nausea returns, whereupon:

> He started down the stairs, leaning with his right hand against the wall. It seemed to him that some kind of yardman with a book in his hand bumped into him, making his way up to the office; that some mutt began barking continuously on a lower floor; that some woman threw a rolling pin at it and shouted.

As Raskolnikov weakly descends the stairs, abandoning his inspiration to confess, the barking and woman's shouting (which recall the howls, moans, and groans in the dream of his landlady, beaten on the stairs) suggest the strident remonstrations of his conscience, which Sonya has helped to awaken. At this point, he reaches the yard where Sonya is waiting. Raskolnikov stops before her. Then, seeing her desperate, tortured expression, he returns up the stairway and confesses.

If seen metaphorically, Raskolnikov begins the novel by "descending" a staircase (with thoughts of his intended crime) and ends it by "ascending" a staircase to confess. As with Mr. Golyadkin at his doctor's, Raskolnikov's three-stage vacillation prior to confessing reflects his ambivalence with regard to seeking help. Mr. Golyadkin's staircase degradation extended, as we have seen, even below the ground. Raskolnikov is struck by extreme revulsion while descending the stairs following his rehearsal visit to Alyona Ivanovna (12), whereupon he continues to descend "on a staircase beneath the sidewalk" to a basement saloon.

After Raskolnikov tells Sonya of his decision to confess, he descends the stairs wondering if it is still possible "not to go" (548). Remembering her words, however, he kisses the earth; then, catching a glimpse of her in the square, he begins his ascent to the police station.

Sonya, we are told, had greatly feared that instead of confessing, Raskolnikov would commit suicide (546). Prior to *his* suicide, Svidrigailov dreams of "a bright, cool staircase covered with luxurious carpeting and lined with rare flowers in Chinese vases" (530). Some of the flowers have a strong, aromatic fragrance, and he finds it difficult to leave them. Nevertheless, Svidrigailov ascends the staircase and beholds the body of a young girl who had killed herself after he abused her. This is followed by his haunting dream of the five-year-old prostitute and his own suicide.

Stairs also lead to death (and near death) in *The Idiot*. As we have seen in the preceding chapter, the painting envisioned by Prince Myshkin of a man condemned to be guillotined anticipates his own near death beneath Rogozhin's "descending" knife. In his proposed painting, the Prince explains, "A short flight of stairs leads to the scaffold." The prisoner "suddenly began crying before the stairs" (6:75). "At the bottom of the stairs he was pale, but when he climbed to the scaffold he suddenly turned white as paper . . ."

It is on Rogozhin's stone steps that he and Myshkin exchange crosses (251), and it is on the stone steps of Myshkin's hotel that Rogozhin attempts to murder him. These steps are dark and narrow; they wind around a thick stone column with a niche in which Rogozhin hides. Myshkin recognizes him by the eyes that flash in the darkness, but he is saved only by an epileptic fit that causes Rogozhin to "freeze on the spot." The Prince falls over backwards, "straight down the stairs, striking the back of his head forcefully against a stone step" (267). His spasms and convulsions carry him all the way to the bottom of the staircase, while Rogozhin rushes down the stairs and leaves. At the end of the novel, just before Myshkin learns that Rogozhin has murdered Nastasia Filippovna, he approaches "the familiar place," thinking: "What if he suddenly comes out of that corner now, and stops me by the stairs?" (682)

In *The Devils*, when Shatov's wife returns to him, he runs "headlong down his steep stairs" to meet her (7:590). "Quickly, Marie," he says. "Easy, we have to go up here . . . the stairs are steep, hold tight, hold tight. . . ." Shatov's words are unwittingly apt: he is unaware that his wife will soon give birth to a child by Stavrogin. Her ascent is thus difficult for various reasons. Shortly thereafter, Shatov reveals to Erkel on the same staircase that his wife has returned (596)—and, we are told, it was this revelation on the stairs (599) that facilitated the murder of Shatov.

At the end of the novel, Stavrogin climbs the stairs to the "attic" (*svetyolka*) and hangs himself. Just before this, he writes to Dasha, suggesting that Kirillov committed suicide "magnanimously," but that he was dedicated to his idea to the point of insanity. "I know that I ought to kill myself," Stavrogin writes, "but I am afraid of suicide because I am afraid of showing magnanimity. I know that it would be yet another deception—the last deception in an endless series of deceptions." (702) For a person in such a frame of mind, the decision to commit suicide could be likened to climbing a (painfully) long, (morally) narrow, terribly steep staircase. And this is precisely what Stavrogin does: "It was necessary to climb almost to the roof on a wooden, long, very narrow, and terribly steep staircase." (703) Varvara Petrovna and Dasha soon rush up this staircase and find Stavrogin's body (704).

Arkadi, the hero of *The Adolescent*, lives in an "attic" (Dostoevsky uses the same word as with Stavrogin, *svetyolka*), and this attic is closely associated with Arkadi's cherished "idea" of amassing riches. "I lived up in an attic, under the roof; I climbed up there by an exceedingly steep and creaky staircase." (8:109) Arkadi frequently withdraws into this room, with its "terribly low ceiling," which can be likened to his "withdrawing into" (18) his idea.[6]

Early in the novel, Arkadi blurts out some bitter reproaches about

Versilov and retreats in agitation to his room: "He had decisively never come to my attic, but suddenly—I hadn't yet been there an hour—I heard his steps on the stairs. . . ." (135) Their long conversation fails to reconcile them; but later, when Versilov visits Arkadi in his rented room, they are touchingly brought together as Versilov leaves. "These staircases," he says, as if to prevent Arkadi from speaking, "these stairs . . . I'll find the way . . . Don't bother. . . ." (229)

> But I didn't leave. We were already descending the second flight.
> "I was waiting for you these whole three days," I suddenly blurted out. It came out by itself. I was panting.
> "Thank you, my dear boy."

As Versilov opens the outer door, the wind blows out Arkadi's candle. Seizing Versilov's hand, he kisses it "many times, fervently." Versilov, his voice shaking, asks why Arkadi loves him so much. Unable to answer, Arkadi rushes back up the stairs to his room, where he weeps with happiness. The final staircase incident in the novel, however, is a tragic one: Arkadi's sister falls on the stairs and has a miscarriage (618).

In *The Brothers Karamazov*, when Ivan suspects in horror that Smerdyakov considers himself in league with him, he performs what he later deems "the most despicable act of his entire life" (9:347). Ivan, we are told, "came out on the stairs" at night to listen to his father, who was waiting expectantly below. Ivan "listened for a long time, for about five minutes, with some kind of strange curiosity, holding his breath, his heart pounding." He "walked out on the stairs" for that purpose "about two times." This episode later haunts Ivan "continuously" (10:130) and he even recalls it "for the hundredth time" (138), concluding that he had "wanted the murder."

The next morning, Ivan tells Smerdyakov that he is off to Chermashnya, whereupon the latter ominously but ambiguously suggests that things are going as planned: "It's interesting to talk with an intelligent person." (351) After seeing Ivan off, Fyodor Pavlovich is distressed by the following event: "Smerdyakov went to the cellar for something and fell downwards from the top step." Marfa Ignatevna, we are told, "did not see the falling," but she heard "the cry of an epileptic, falling in a fit."

> Whether his fit occurred at the very moment that he was going down the steps, so that he, of course, must have immediately fallen headlong, unconscious, or whether

the fit of Smerdyakov, a well-known epileptic, resulted from the impact of his fall—it was impossible to discern, but he was already on the cellar floor when they found him, frothing at the mouth and writhing in spasms and convulsions.

This vivid description (which questions only why—not whether—Smerdyakov fell) tends to obscure the potentially suspicious fact that Marfa only heard, but did not see, the falling. Indeed, if we believe what Smerdyakov later tells Ivan, he "walked quietly down the stairs, sir, to the very bottom, sir, and lay down quietly, sir, and when I lay down, I began yelling." (10:148) It thus seems practically certain that the most dramatic stairway episode in the novel, a crucial accompaniment to the murder of Fyodor Karamazov, never actually occurred. Nonetheless, Dostoevsky strategically re-evokes the scene: at Mitya's trial, the prosecutor persuasively describes Smerdyakov, in an epileptic seizure, "flying headlong" to the bottom of the cellar stairs (10:255).

All this may be compared to *The Idiot*, wherein Prince Myshkin does indeed have an epileptic fit on a staircase. Whereas Myshkin's fit (when he says, "Parfyon, I don't believe it!") saves him from being killed, Smerdyakov's "fit" saves him from being found guilty of killing. (Once again, if we believe Smerdyakov, he soon had a "genuine" fit that aided his deception.) Moreover, Myshkin is ascending while he is saved, whereas Smerdyakov is descending (after his timely fit, he becomes disillusioned and commits suicide).

Falling on a staircase is—to use Bitsilli's term—quite "terrifying," but falling on the stairs in the throes of an epileptic fit is still more dramatically so. Like Myshkin's, Smerdyakov's epilepsy is repeatedly termed *paduchaya bolezn'* ("falling sickness"), and at the crucial moment, he is described as "falling in a fit" (*padayushchego v pripadke*)—which doubly reflects the root meaning of his epilepsy. And at the trial (10:254), the prosecutor pictures him "falling in epilepsy" (*upadaet v paduchej bolezni*). Obviously, such effects resist translation.

As noted above, when Madame Khokhlakova rushes out to meet Alyosha on the stairs, she suggests a parallel with the climactic stairway episode in Griboedov's *Woe from Wit*: she is Famusov, Alyosha is Chatsky, and Lisa is Sofya. In *The Adolescent*, Arkadi recalls that he first met Versilov when the latter was declaiming Chatsky's monologue: "A carriage for me, a carriage!" (8:124) Arkadi declares that he had caught a glimpse of Versilov the day before, "on the stairs, but only in passing. You were going down the stairs to get in a carriage. . . ." In Griboedov's play,

Chatsky returns to Sofya (Pavlovna) from abroad but does not marry her—a sequence of events that fits Versilov and Sofya Andreevna.[7]

As we have seen, some of Dostoevsky's most dramatic scenes are (in P. M. Bitsilli's phrase) "exceedingly often played out on staircases." Indeed, Dostoevskian stairways become dynamic stage settings for vivid episodes: pursuit, escape, concealment, violence, falling, and cold, protracted, painful isolation. From Varenka's stairway degradations in *Poor People* to Madame Khokhlakova's observation that she, Lisa, and Alyosha Karamazov resemble characters in *Woe from Wit*, where "everything fateful happened on the stairs," we have traced the details that characteristically intensify these episodes. Some details—for example, a pounding heart— serve to reveal or reinforce a character's emotions. Others—for instance, a slamming door, reflecting the jolt of a painful separation—function metaphorically. At times, the characters' very actions and situations become metaphorically suggestive: Mr. Golyadkin's quite literal degradations in *The Double*, the difficult ascent of Shatov's wife (*The Devils*), Raskolnikov's rising to confess at the end of *Crime and Punishment*. Most strikingly, perhaps, several stairway episodes immediately precede or focus upon murder, near death, or suicide.

Notes

1. Ivanov's opinion, as well as the objection of M. M. Bakhtin, are discussed by P. M. Bitsilli, "K voprosu o vnutrennei forme romana Dostoevskogo," *O Dostoevskom: Stat'i* (Providence, R.I., 1966), pp. 10–11. See also p. 47.

George Steiner persuasively argues that Dostoevsky's four major novels contain "the architecture and substance of drama." (*Tolstoy or Dostoevsky: An Essay in The Old Criticism*, New York, 1961, p. 136.)

2. Steiner, pp. 140, 159, respectively.

3. Bitsilli, p. 53. According to Andrew Field, Bitsilli was "Nabokov's own favorite Russian critic of his work." (*VN: The Life and Art of Vladimir Nabokov*, New York, 1986, p. 146.)

4. The Russian is *chyornaya* (literally, "black" stairs). The same term is used for the stairs by which Raskolnikov reaches Alyona Ivanovna's apartment in *Crime and Punishment* (5:8) and, in *The Idiot*, for the stairs by which General Ivolgin must enter and leave his quarters (6:104).

5. Netochka, Nelli, and Vanya are discussed below. In *White Nights*, Nastenka walks on the stairs "for a whole hour" (2:36) before visiting the man for whom her passion has developed in several stairway encounters (33, 35). And in *The Devils*, when Shatov's wife

returns, he stands at the top of the stairs "for about ten minutes," his head pressed into a corner (7:595–6).

6. Here one may recall Vanya's observation in *The Insulted and The Injured* that "in a cramped room, even one's thoughts are cramped" (3:7). Versilov defines Arkadi's small room as "a coffin, a perfect coffin!" (8:135)

7. One is tempted to conjecture that Dostoevsky intended to have Alyosha Karamazov travel abroad and then return to, but not marry, Lisa Khokhlakova.

9

Dostoevskian Smiles

The term "body language" sooner recalls Tolstoy, and an entire article has been devoted to smiling in *Anna Karenina*.[1] Yet eloquent smiles—often quite unusual ones—regularly occur at important moments in Dostoevsky's works. Here we shall trace such smiles and examine their effects. Examples will be limited to the noun *ulybka* ("smile"), its diminutive *ulybochka*,[2] and the verb *ulybat'sya* ("to smile").

First, however, let us examine a brief sampling of Dostoevskian smiles. Some are vividly imaginative: "on his lips was the very sweetest of his customary smiles, which usually recalled vinegar with sugar" (7:492). Many are unpleasant, painful: "distorting his mouth into a convulsive smile" (2:585); "smiling hysterically" (2:104); "a heavy, astonished smile burdensomely, as if with pain, pressed itself out upon her lips" (1:486). Many are malicious, even sinister: "with a poisoned, maliciously derisive smile" (3:451); "with a murderous smile" (1:244); "in his smile I discerned something exceedingly vile, shady, and sinister" (8:164). Some are complex mixtures: "in his pale, still similarly twisted-from-fright smile there suddenly flashed something as if sly, even triumphant" (6:437); "He blissfully smiled, although in his smile there seemed to be reflected something full of suffering or, better to say, something humane, supreme." (8:506) As we shall find, however, purely pleasant smiles are relatively rare.

As *Crime and Punishment* begins, Raskolnikov finds it odd that he fears meeting his landlady—considering what he has planned to do. He thinks this, we are told, "with a strange smile." (5:6) This is the first, mysterious reference to Raskolnikov's crime. Later, he tauntingly asks Zamiotov: "And what if it was I who killed the old woman and Lizaveta?" Zamiotov gapes "wildly," his face "distorted by a smile" (173). In *The*

Brothers Karamazov, when Ivan admits "instructing" Smerdyakov to commit the murder, Dmitri's reaction is remarkably similar: "Mitya . . . stared
and listened to his brother with some kind of wild, distorted smile."
(10:226)

Later in *Crime and Punishment*, when Raskolnikov hints to Sonya
that he is the murderer (427–8), his smiles are "pale," "distorted," and
repeatedly "strengthless." Then, as Sonya realizes the truth, her expression
of childlike terror—said to resemble Lizaveta's, when Raskolnikov killed
her—seems to transmit itself to Raskolnikov's own face: he looks at her
with "the very same fear" and "almost even with the very same *childlike*
smile." This tends to unite Lizaveta, Sonya, and Raskolnikov much as the
reading of Lizaveta's Bible is to do later, suggesting that all three are
children before God.[3] Finally, at the police station, Raskolnikov hesitates
and looks at Sonya, whereupon: "An ugly, lost smile pressed itself out
upon his lips." (556) He then officially admits that he is the murderer,
completing a series of three "confessions," variously intensified by unusual
smiles. The final one (*Bezobraznaya, poteryannaya ulybka vydavilas' na ego
ustakh*) is particularly difficult to translate. Three standard versions are:

> A ghastly, lost smile forced its way to his lips.
> A forlorn, ghastly smile hovered over Raskolnikov's lips.
> He forced himself to smile, a lost, hideous smile.[4]

One problem is that the word *bezobraznaya* can mean both "ugly" and
"vague, without shape." Still another translation reads: "His lips worked
in an ugly, meaningless smile."[5]

Late in the novel, Svidrigailov declares to Raskolnikov that Dunya is
the sort of martyr who "would surely smile while her breast was being
burned with red-hot tongs" (496). This image ominously intensifies the
confrontation scene that follows. As Dunya tries desperately to open the
locked door, "a malicious and mocking smile" slowly appears on Svidrigailov's "still trembling lips" (516). And: "The mocking smile did not leave
him." Finally, convinced that Dunya will not submit, but still not trusting
himself, Svidrigailov gives her the key and she rushes out: "A strange smile
distorted his face, a pitiful, sad, weak smile, a smile of despair." He picks
up the revolver and leaves.

Prior to his suicide, Svidrigailov dreams of two young girls. The first
is a fourteen-year-old who drowned herself after he sexually abused her:
"the smile on her pale lips was full of some kind of unchildlike, boundless

sorrow and supreme grievance." (531) The other child, who seems no more than five years old, horrifies Svidrigailov as her "little lips widen in a smile" and she laughs in the manner of a seasoned prostitute (533). The shocking incongruity of this tiny girl's smile reflects Svidrigailov's perverted sexual preference, while her laughter suggests the nightmare-distorted reaction of his conscience to the first victim's outraged smile: "There was something infinitely ugly and insulting in that laughter. . . ."

In *The Idiot*, Rogozhin's smile reflects the duality of his nature and his ambivalent attitude towards Prince Myshkin. In the opening train scene, Rogozhin's lips "continually" form "some kind of impudent, mocking, and even malicious smile" (6:6). His face, however, has an "agonizingly passionate" quality "that did not harmonize with his coarse, insolent smile." Later, when Myshkin visits him, Rogozhin "twists" his mouth "into some kind of exceedingly perplexed smile, as if he found something impossible and almost miraculous in the Prince's visit." (232) Then, when Myshkin suggests that Rogozhin has been stalking him in the crowd, Rogozhin evasively replies that Myshkin may have imagined it: "The affectionate smile on his face did not suit him at that moment, as if something had become broken in that smile and Parfyon was quite unable to glue it back together no matter how hard he tried." Not long after this, Rogozhin raises his knife above Myshkin—"a furious smile distorted his face" (266)—but the Prince has an epileptic seizure and survives. Finally, when Rogozhin leads Myshkin to the body of Nastasia Filippovna, he has a "sly and almost satisfied smile" (684).

Prince Myshkin has one of the few genuinely positive smiles in all of Dostoevsky's works. When he calls upon General Epanchin, his smile is "so devoid of any hint of any kind of hidden inimical feeling" that the suspicious General regards him entirely differently (30) and soon smiles "merrily" himself. As Ippolit declares of Myshkin: "He has a good smile; I've studied him more closely now." (439) Even when Ganya furiously slaps the Prince's face, Myshkin's expression shows no anger or malice: "his lips trembled and tried to utter something; some kind of strange and inappropriate smile was twisting them." (135) Myshkin explains that it was essential to prevent Ganya from striking his sister. "Oh, how ashamed you will be of your behavior!" Myshkin exclaims, and his face soon displays "the very same inappropriate smile." As this smile may suggest, Myshkin's rare capacity for empathy has given him a prophetic insight into Ganya's painful, beneficial repentance for his shameful conduct.[6]

Other Dostoevskian characters with positive smiles are also percep-
tively compassionate. In "Peasant Marey," the title figure (who comforts a
frightened little boy) has a smile that is first "worried," then repeatedly
"maternal" and "tender" (10:368–70). And in Ivan Karamazov's story of
The Grand Inquisitor, Christ walks among the people "with a quiet smile
of infinite compassion" (9:312). George Steiner has suggested that Dostoevsky's own "position" with respect to Ivan's fable "is gathered into the
silence of Christ; it is realized not in language, but in a single gesture—the
kiss which Christ bestows on the Inquisitor."[7] If Christ's kiss "answers" the
Grand Inquisitor, should not Christ's "quiet smile of infinite compassion"
be understood as a silent, loving reply to the terrible existence of Ivan's
child victims? Is this not to place, as Dostoevsky insistently preferred,
Christ above the truth?

Dostoevskian babies and little children also have genuinely positive
smiles—at least, until they have been exposed to cruelty and suffering.
Significantly, it is Prince Myshkin who compares a mother's joy in observing her baby's first smile to God's joy when, from heaven, He observes a
sinner praying to Him with his entire heart (6:250). In *The Diary of a
Writer* for 1876, Dostoevsky describes his own encounter with a woman
prisoner who smiled when asked about her newborn daughter: "This smile
of a mother sentenced to penal servitude, directed at her baby, who was
born in the stockade just after her sentencing, a sentencing which, even
before she appeared in the world, condemned her together with her
mother—this smile produced in me a strange and oppressive sensation."[8]

In *The Devils*, Dostoevsky employed unusual smiles to reflect
Stavrogin's enigmatic nature. Immediately after his odd prank of leading
Gaganov by the nose, Stavrogin "not only was not embarrassed, but, on the
contrary, smiled maliciously and merrily" (7:48). This is combined with
the observation that he seemed to feel no repentance whatsoever.

When Stavrogin's mother asks him directly if Marya Timofeevna is his
lawful wife, he stares at her fixedly, with no change of expression: "Finally,
he slowly smiled some kind of indulgent smile. . . ." (194) Then, after
kissing his mother's hand, Stavrogin walks over to Marya Timofeevna, who
asks if she may kneel down before him. He tells her that she may not,
"smiling magnificently so that she immediately grinned with joy." Much
later, when his "rival" Mavriki Nikolaevich visits him, a smile flashes on
Stavrogin's lips—"a smile of arrogant triumph and at the same time of
some kind of vacant, distrustful amazement." (399) As this complex smile

suggestively anticipates, Mavriki Nikolaevich asks Stavrogin to marry Lizaveta Nikolaevna; Stavrogin reveals that he is already married. Finally, when Lizaveta herself asks about the Lebyadkins, Stavrogin answers that he has been Marya Timofeevna's husband for almost five years. He then smiles "with boundless arrogance" (478) and leaves the room.

In *The Brothers Karamazov*, Dostoevsky used eloquent smiles to hint at the impending murder of Fyodor Pavlovich. When Alyosha asks Ivan "how it will end" between Dmitri and their father, Ivan angrily replies that he is not his brother Dmitri's "watchman," but then: "he suddenly somehow bitterly smiled." (9:290) Ivan also "suddenly" smiles at a crucial point in the Grand Inquisitor legend: when the Inquisitor says, "Tomorrow I will burn You. *Dixi*." (9:327) Ralph Matlaw has interpreted this smile as evidence that Ivan is an incipient epileptic.[9] Like Ivan's bitter smile about Fyodor Pavlovich, it ominously anticipates murder. Smerdyakov later asks Ivan why he hasn't yet left for Chermashnya—and "smiled familiarly," his squinting left eye seeming to say: "And as for why I smiled, you yourself ought to understand, if you are an intelligent person." (336)

Dostoevsky frequently used tortured smiles to reflect a painful concern about honor. "I cannot marry someone else's sins!" exclaims Stepan Trofimovich in *The Devils*. He says this "with a pitiful and lost smile, a smile of shame and utter despair." (7:113) "You are a passionate person," the (cuckolded) Eternal Husband tells Velchaninov, "somehow especially vilely smiling." (4:485) And in *The Devils*, when Shatov, whom Stavrogin has cuckolded, reminds Stavrogin of the slap in the face that he gave him, Shatov adds: "Again you are smiling your fastidious, fashionable smile." (7:261)

In *Crime and Punishment*, when Raskolnikov learns of the attacks upon his sister's honor: "a bitter, malicious smile writhed upon his lips" (5:44). A more literal translation would be: "a heavy, bilious, spiteful smile stole across his lips," but *zmeilas'* ("stole") also suggests the action of a snake.[10] Following Nastasia Filippovna's "maidenly shame" (*The Idiot*), even though plans are made for her to marry Ganya, Totsky fears that there may still be "a snake beneath the flowers" (6:57). Then, when Myshkin reproaches Nastasia for her outrageous conduct at Ganya's, she appears to be "hiding something beneath her smile" (136)—a subtle reflection of the earlier image. Ganya's honor is variously tested in the novel, and as he stares at the flaming package of money: "An insane smile wandered over his pale-as-a-sheet face." (199)

In *The Brothers Karamazov* Grushenka, who has also suffered "maidenly shame," asks Alyosha if, in his opinion, she still loves her "offender." He replies that she has forgotten the man, and, although she agrees: "A suggestion of cruelty flashed in her smile." (9:444)[11] She then bitterly complains that he is whistling for her to come crawling like a little dog—her face "warped by a sickly smile" (446). "I'll show you a little trick now, sir!" Captain Snegiryov tells Alyosha "with the look of someone who has decided to jump from a cliff and, at the same time, as if smiling with his lips." Then he tramples the money he so desperately needs, declaring that his honor is not for sale. (9:265–6)

Some Dostoevskian smiles are said to be uncharacteristic or even unprecedented. In *The Insulted and The Injured,* after Natasha abandons her parents to live with Alyosha, Vanya notices, in her smile, "something full of suffering, tender, patient." (3:85) Natasha then calls Vanya "Alyosha" and smiles at her mistake.

> "I'm looking at your smile now, Natasha. Where did you get it? You didn't have one like that before."
> "And what is there in my smile?"
> "Well, it still has the same childlike open-heartedness . . . But when you smile, it's as if something aches strongly in your heart." (3:91)

In this early novel, Natasha's unprecedented smile reflects her conviction that she is "condemned to sacrifice for her love," as Ernest Simmons has put it.[12] In *The Brothers Karamazov,* Ivan suddenly smiles

> . . . exactly like a timid little boy. Never before had Alyosha seen him have such a smile. (9:296)

At this point, Ivan begins his story of outrageous child victims that seem to justify returning one's "ticket" to God. Ivan's uncharacteristic smile thus allies him with the children he is about to describe, intensifying both his, and the reader's emotional involvement. Frank Silbajoris has remarked that ". . . as Ivan begins to talk about the tortures of children, . . . he seems to identify himself with the children, to become, as it were, a suffering child himself."[13] Ivan's tale of a little boy torn to pieces by hunting dogs before his mother's eyes elicits from Alyosha the following judgment upon the general who ordered the massacre:

> "Shoot him!" Alyosha quietly declared, looking up at his brother with some kind of pale, warped smile. (305)

Alyosha's uncharacteristically harsh verdict is persuasively reflected in his uncharacteristic smile.

In *The Adolescent*, the conversation in which Versilov informs Arkadi that Anna Andreevna plans to marry "your sweet little old man" (8:329) begins as follows:

> "I thought you'd come here," he said, smiling strangely and strangely looking at me. His smile was unkind, and I had not seen one like that on his face for a long time.

The word *nedobraya* ("unkind") can also mean "bad" or even "evil." Versilov's unusual smile thus tends to anticipate what Arkadi terms his "derisive" revelation of Anna Andreevna's conniving plan and the old Prince's "ecstatic" reaction to "her" marriage proposal.

Dostoevskian smiles are sometimes depicted as unforgettable, even haunting. In Stavrogin's "Confession" (*The Devils*), he recalls making advances to Matryosha: "Here she suddenly drew back and smiled with shame, but it was some kind of crooked smile."[14] The girl then abruptly, avidly kisses Stavrogin. Finally, after he seduces Matryosha, and she kills herself: "My main hatred was at the recollection of her smile." (53)

The Underground Man recalls lighting a match in the dark bedroom with Liza: "What a pitiful, what an unnatural, what a distorted smile she had at that moment!" (4:226) "Fifteen years later," he adds, "I would still picture Liza precisely with that pitiful, distorted, unnecessary smile." The modifiers of Liza's haunting smile anticipate the Underground Man's sermonized view of her life as unnatural, distorted, pitiful, and unnecessary.

The smile of the heroine in "A Timid Creature" serves a more clearly prophetic function: "I suddenly saw a smile—distrustful, taciturn, bad. It was with this very smile that I led her into my house." (10:391) Just before her suicide, the girl smiles "strangely"—"so strangely" that Lukerya returns to find her "smiling, standing, thinking and smiling" (416)—after which she hurls herself from the window to her death.

As we have seen, Dostoevsky frequently punctuated important moments in his works with complex, unusual smiles. Having examined some of their effects in context, we may now offer a few generalizations. Dostoevskian smiles are predominantly unpleasant. Several are described as unforgettable, uncharacteristic, or even unprecedented. Tortured smiles typically reflect a harbored insult or humiliation—most often, a painful concern about one's honor. The preponderance of unpleasant, disharmonious, or enigmatic smiles can perhaps be explained, in part, by the following passage from *The Adolescent*. Though Arkadi's words refer to "laughter" (*smekh*), they apply to many of the Dostoevskian smiles discussed above.

> I think that when a person laughs, it becomes in most cases disgusting to look at him. . . . Laughter requires sincerity first of all, and where is there sincerity in people? . . . I only know that laughter is the truest test of the soul. Look at a child: only children can laugh with perfect goodness—that's why they are so captivating. (8:389–91)

Arkadi finds various adult smiles highly unpleasant throughout the novel,[15] and his theory revealingly contrasts with the opinion of Tolstoy's narrator in *Childhood:*

> It seems to me that in the smile alone consists what is called the beauty of a face: if the smile adds charm to a face, the face is beautiful; if it does not alter it, it is ordinary; if it spoils it, it is ugly. (1:17)

The two passages tend to recall Tolstoy's reputation as a "seer of the flesh" and Dostoevsky's as a "seer of the spirit." Whereas Tolstoy's vision focuses initially on physical attractiveness, Dostoevsky's immediate concern is with sincerity and the soul. For Tolstoy, a smile can either guarantee or spoil the beauty of a face; the effect of Dostoevskian smiles is predominantly negative. Indeed, Dostoevsky's use of strange, complex smiles reflects his preoccupation with the tortuous convolutions of the human psyche. Except for Christ, Prince Myshkin, the idealized peasant Marey, and a few still-innocent children,[16] Dostoevsky's characters display smiles that reveal a scarring by suffering and a tainting by evil.

Notes

1. Michael Pursglove, "The Smiles of *Anna Karenina*," *Slavic and East European Journal*, Vol. 17, No. 1 (Spring 1973), 42–48.

2. The effect of this form, signifying "little smile" with suggestions of "dear," "cute," "sweet," etc., can vary considerably in context. "Little smiles" are exhibited by such diverse people as police inspector Porfiry Petrovich (*Crime and Punishment*), the scheming suitor in "The Fir Tree and The Wedding," and both Mr. Golyadkins (*The Double*).

3. See my *Dostoevsky: Child and Man in His Works* (New York, 1968), p. 176.

4. Sidney Monas (New York, 1968), p. 510; David Magarshack (New York, 1966), p. 542; and Jessie Coulson (New York, 1964), p. 510—respectively.

5. Constance Garnett (New York, 1962), p. 457.

6. In Edward Wasiolek's view: "By suffering the slap, by 'absorbing' the hurt, the Prince brings Ganya to remorse and even to love." (*Dostoevsky: The Major Fiction*, Cambridge, 1964, p. 104.)

7. George Steiner, *Tolstoy or Dostoevsky* (New York, 1961), p. 342.

8. F. M. Dostoevskii, *Dnevnik pisatelya za 1876 god* (Paris, YMCA-Press), p. 462.

9. Ralph E. Matlaw, *The Brothers Karamazov: Novelistic Technique* (The Hague, 1957), p. 36.

10. Monas has: "A heavy, bilious, angry smile played around his lips." (p. 47) Magarshack: "a bitter, spiteful, evil smile played on his lips." (p. 57) Garnett: "a bitter, wrathful and malignant smile was on his lips." (p. 35) Coulson has, simply: "a bitter angry smile played over his lips." (p. 37) The Russian is: *tyazhyolaya, zhyolchnaya, zlaya ulybka zmeilas' po ego gubam*.

11. Dostoevsky's Russian is vivid but vague, literally: "Some kind of cruel little characteristic was fleetingly apparent in her smile." Andrew MacAndrew has: "There was a hint of cruelty in her slightly twisted smile." (New York, 1972, p. 431.)

12. Ernest J. Simmons, *Dostoevsky: The Making of a Novelist* (New York, 1962), p. 102.

13. Rimvydas Silbajoris, "The Children in *The Brothers Karamazov*," *The Slavic and East European Journal*, Vol. VII, No. 1 (Spring 1963), p. 30.

14. F. M. Dostoevskii, *U Tikhona* (New York, 1964), p. 50.

15. See pp. 152, 160, 246, 308, 418, 459.

16. Katerina Nikolaevna (in *The Adolescent*) may seem to be an exception. Arkadi describes her smile at great length (8:274–7), exclaiming: "I cannot endure your smile!" and "I cannot endure your smile any longer!" Yet for him, her face is pure and innocent as a child's. "I love the way you never stop smiling," he tells her. "It's—my paradise!" However, Katerina is by no means as pure as Arkadi believes. In Wasiolek's words, "Katerina is revealed finally to be a selfish, somewhat sadistic, and even trivial woman." (p. 140)

10

The Fourfold Orientation of *Fathers and Sons*

David Lowe has observed that parallelism and contrast are the two basic principles at work in *Fathers and Sons*.[1] Remarkably often, this seems to promote effects of quadruplicity in the novel—a pattern that extends from structural organization to a variety of individual details. Indeed, Turgenev's creative vision seems ultimately to have been directed towards a fourfold orientation.

Turgenev's title refers, nongenerically, to four people: Arkadi, Bazarov, and their fathers. The novel takes place at four locations:

1) the Kirsanovs'
2) the town of ***
3) Madame Odintsova's
4) the Bazarovs'

At each location, four people are featured (Arkadi and Bazarov plus two others):

1) Nikolai Petrovich, Pavel Petrovich
2) Kukshkina, Sitnikov
3) Odintsova, Katya
4) Bazarov's parents

Richard Freeborn has suggested that each of these locations, with its occupants, serves to illuminate an aspect of Bazarov:

1) Pavel Petrovich, Bazarov's ideological significance
2) Sitnikov and Kukshina, Bazarov's superiority within his generation
3) Odintsova, the duality in Bazarov's nature
4) Bazarov's parents, his egoism and individual insignificance[2]

Virginia Burns has detected the following pattern in four sections of the novel: first, the setting, the characters, and their relationships are defined; then the action rises to a climax, after which it drops off quickly.[3]

1) At Marino, the climax is Pavel's quarrel with Bazarov.

2) At Nikolskoe, it is Bazarov's declaration of his feelings to Odintsova.

3) At the Bazarovs', it is Arkadi's and Bazarov's quarrel.

4) At Marino, it is the duel between Pavel and Bazarov.

Bazarov figures in each "climax," and the fourth section functions as a projection of the first.

Freeborn has noted that the novel contains four different love stories:

1) Nikolai—Fenechka

2) Pavel—Fenechka, involving Bazarov

3) Bazarov—Odintsova

4) Arkadi—Katya[4]

Lowe points up a different fourfold pattern by observing that the love stories of Arkadi and Bazarov can be fully appreciated and understood only when compared to those of Nikolai Petrovich and Pavel Petrovich. (He refers to Pavel's previous relationship with Princess R. and Nikolai's love for his first wife and for Fenechka.[5])

Another quadruple grouping results from the fact that Nikolai Petrovich's marriage to Arkadi's mother "coincided" with Pavel Petrovich's meeting Princess R., particularly because both women died at about the same time (3:145).

Charles Moser has observed that the novel's primary ideological opponents, Bazarov and Pavel Petrovich, are quite similar in many facets of their emotional and psychological make-up.[6] Joel Blair has noted that Bazarov's description of Pavel Petrovich (staking his whole life on the card of a woman's love and then, when that card fails, turning sour and letting himself go till he's fit for nothing) later fits Bazarov's own life. He also suggests that Odintsova is a "realistic version" of the "melodramatic caricature" Princess R.[7] All this suggests the fourfold relationship: Bazarov is to Odintsova as Pavel Petrovich is to Princess R. Among other parallel details, Princess R.'s love for Pavel Petrovich is termed a fire that finally goes out forever (145); at the end, Bazarov tells Odintsova to "blow on the dying lamp: let it go out" (271).

If, as Lowe suggests, the duel between Bazarov and Pavel Petrovich "displays the depth of Pavel's attraction to Fenechka, who reminds him of Princess R.,"[8] we may note that the duel also follows Bazarov's rejection by Odintsova. It is thus fought between two analogous characters who have recently "lost" two other analogous characters. Blair has proposed that "the grouping and regrouping of characters" is the novel's primary compositional principle.[9]

This can be related to another quadruple grouping: ". . . just as the wounded Bazarov takes refuge in a flirtation with Fenechka—a romance which he knows cannot really touch his bruised ego, so the chastened Odintsova focuses on a much less dangerous male of the species, Arkady."[10]

Another fourfold grouping emerges if we see "Sitnikov as Bazarov's parodic double and Kukshina as Odintsova's."[11] This leads briefly to still another. When Sitnikov, outraged at being snubbed by Arkadi and Bazarov, returns to Kukshkina's: "the two 'disgusting stuck-up dolts' were harshly criticized." (204) Standard translations have Sitnikov alone do the criticizing[12]; at the ball, however, Kukshina's pride had been "deeply wounded" when both Arkadi and Bazarov ignored her (178). She therefore presumably joined in the name-calling.

Four peasant figures at the Kirsanovs' estate play significant roles in their own right: Pyotr, Prokofich, Fenechka, and Dunyasha (Bazarov, without suspecting it, becomes the "cruel tyrant" of her heart, p. 230). Also at the Kirsanovs', the main quadruplicity is symmetrically doubled: Bazarov evaluates the two "old men" for Arkadi; Pavel Petrovich passes judgment on the two young men to Nikolai Petrovich.

When Arkadi leaves Bazarov at the Kirsanovs', he is replaced in the quadruple focus by Fenechka.

Early in the novel, Arkadi declares that Bazarov is a "nihilist," and this is followed by four interpretations of the word. Nikolai Petrovich suggests that it signifies a person "who recognizes nothing." "Who respects nothing," declares Pavel Petrovich. In Arkadi's view, it is someone "who looks at everything critically." (139) And in Bazarov's, someone who "denies everything." (159)

Late in the novel, Bazarov declares to Odintsova that "love is an imaginary feeling" (253). "Really?" she replies. "I'm very pleased to hear that." Shortly thereafter, Odintsova addresses Arkadi and Katya: "Children! Tell me, is love an imaginary feeling?" (260) "But neither Katya nor Arkadi," we are told, "even understood her." The word "imaginary" is *napusknoe* (literally, "put on") in both instances, and the reader may be tempted to associate the attitudes of these four people towards love, whether self-fulfilling or not, with their degree of success in finding it.

The same four characters are grouped in a single sentence by their feelings about nature: "Katya *adored* nature, and Arkadi loved it, although he did not dare to admit this; Odintsova was quite indifferent to it, and so was Bazarov." (189–190)

Fathers and Sons contains four important instances of eavesdropping or overhearing:

1) Nikolai Petrovich overhears Bazarov tell Arkadi that he, Nikolai Petrovich, is a "good fellow," but "his song has been sung." (155)

2) Bazarov overhears his father ask about where he is (and perhaps considerably more); Arkadi has just concluded his "opinion" of Bazarov by assuring the old man that he will be "famous" (215).

3) Pavel Petrovich overhears Bazarov flirting with Fenechka (233).

4) Arkadi and Katya overhear Bazarov and Odintsova (256–7).

On all four occasions, the characters are in gardens. In three cases, the listeners overhear words about themselves; in the other one, Pavel Petrovich overhears Bazarov expressing feelings for Fenechka that he, Pavel, may share.

We see Pavel Petrovich in four reflective poses:

1) After meeting Bazarov, he stares at the "quivering flame" of the fire with an expression of gloomy concentration (136).

2) Upon hearing that Bazarov is a "nihilist," he remains "motionless," holding aloft his butter-laiden knife (139).

3) Having visited Fenechka and remarked that her baby resembles his brother, he remains "motionless" on the sofa, hands behind his head, staring with desperation at the ceiling (152).

4) After urging his brother to marry Fenechka and adding, "with a melancholy smile," that perhaps Bazarov was right to reproach him for "aristocratism," he closes his eyes, his head on the pillow "like that of a corpse" (246).

In all four cases, and with increasing resignation, Pavel Petrovich seems to be contemplating the disintegration of the values and customs he has always respected.

Turgenev gives us four indications that Bazarov gets on easily with peasants and children. First, he calls a coachman "bushy-beard," and another peasant approvingly agrees (128). Next he talks naturally with two peasant boys, and Turgenev declares that he possessed "the special skills of inspiring the trust of lower-class people" (136). Then Bazarov holds Fenechka's baby, who, to her and to Dunyasha's "amazement," shows neither fear nor resistance (153). Finally, we are told that Fenechka behaves "more freely and easily" with Bazarov than with Nikolai Petrovich himself (229).[13]

In four conversations with Arkadi, Bazarov disparagingly employs the expression *pustyaki* ("trifles, nonsense, rubbish"). His targets are: the Russian people and nature (154), the society of women (205), his own place in the universe (216), and the noble emotions of the gentry (259). The first time, Arkadi becomes disturbed; after the second, Bazarov offends a peasant by asking if his wife beats him; the third time, Bazarov suggests that he and Arkadi fight seriously; the fourth time, he explains that Arkadi "does not fight," whereas he himself "wants to fight."[14]

This pattern overlaps with one of challenging. Pavel Petrovich challenges Bazarov verbally and, later, physically; Odintsova challenges Bazarov to argue (183); and Bazarov challenges Arkadi to fight (219).

Bazarov yawns at four significant points in the novel: when Pavel Petrovich asks him about "Germans" (141), while drinking Kukshina's champagne (174), when his father extols the beauty of nature (211), and while informing his father that he is about to leave (223).

The novel contains four "warm" characters (Katya, Arkadi, Fenechka, Nikolai Petrovich) and four "cold" ones (Bazarov, Pavel Petrovich, Odintsova, the lawyer she marries). Bazarov likens Odintsova's "coldness" to "ice cream" (177) and declares that she has "frozen herself" (180). Thinking of Bazarov, she falls asleep "all pure and cold" (188). The lawyer she eventually marries is said to be "cold as ice" (273). In Fenechka's words, the mere presence of Pavel Petrovich is enough "to drench you with cold water" (230). Prior to his duel with Bazarov, Pavel Petrovich oppresses everyone with his "icy politeness" (236). After the duel, Bazarov remains "cold as ice" towards Pavel Petrovich (242).

The four warm characters marry at the end. Two of the cold ones marry, one dies, and the other, Pavel Petrovich, remains coldly isolated. Except for the lawyer, the cold characters are all seen as lifeless bodies. Bazarov envisions Odintsova on a dissecting-table (180) and likens himself to a "corpse" (257). Pavel Petrovich's head is likened to "the head of a corpse" (246). And, Turgenev adds, "he *was* a corpse."

The novel contains four quite important characters whom we never see: Nikolai Petrovich's first wife, Princess R., and Odintsova's first and second husbands.

David Lowe, in proposing that "all the characters are defined by their

relation to time," arrives at still another quadruple grouping: "At the conclusion of the novel Pavel has lost his past, Bazarov his future, and the
Kirsanovs—father and son—who neither try to counteract time nor ignore
it, continue living in the everlasting present."[15]

The novel has four main characters who are "old" (Arkadi's father and
uncle; Bazarov's parents) and four who are "young" (Arkadi, Bazarov,
Katya, Fenechka). Odintsova, age twenty-nine, considers herself and Bazarov "old" (258); Katya and Arkadi, "young, young" (253). Of course, the
diverse attitudes of old Prokofich and young Pyotr pointedly parallel the
views of their master Nikolai Petrovich and his son Arkadi.

Early in the novel, Bazarov offers his hand to Nikolai Petrovich "not
immediately" (128). Pavel Petrovich avoids offering his hand to Bazarov:
"and even put it back in his pocket." (134) The young servant Pyotr does
not kiss Arkadi's hand (128), but old Prokofich does (133). In combination,
these four attitudes are richly suggestive; Lowe even states that "the issue
of kissing hands or not kissing them explicitly parallels Bazarov's and
Pavel's offering or not offering their hands."[16] Pavel Petrovich does offer
his aristocratic hand (described in detail) to Arkadi, for which Turgenev
inserts the English words "shake hands" into the Russian text—an effect
not apparent in standard translations.[17] English versions also obscure the
fact that Pavel Petrovich's "suit" is indicated by the transliterated, and
italicized, English word *"s'yut"* in this scene and elsewhere. Like the words
"shake hands," this is important because, as we later learn, Pavel Petrovich had "arranged his entire life in the English style" after the death of
Princess R. (146)—and because Pavel Petrovich's *"s'yut"* (230) is em-
blematic, for Fenechka, in sharply distinguishing him (from Bazarov) as
an unnatural person.

Lowe has described what amounts to four "roles" for Arkadi: "his false
role as Bazarov's protegé and a rival for Odintsova" and "his true status as
his father's son and claimant for Katya's hand."[18]

The fourfold orientation of *Fathers and Sons* includes a variety of
apparently unrelated details. Bazarov and Pavel Petrovich agree that their
duel will consist of four shots (235). Bazarov then dreams of four people
(Odintsova, his mother, Fenechka, and Pavel Petrovich), and Pyotr awakens him "at four o'clock" in the morning (236–7). Bazarov declares:
"What's important is that two times two is four. All the rest is rubbish."
(154) He and Arkadi return to Odintsova's for "four hours." (This is mentioned twice, p. 225.) Four characters (Arkadi, Bazarov, Kukshina, and

Sitnikov) drink four bottles of champagne together (174). Among other such details,[19] Bazarov's father receives "four eggs" for giving a peasant medical care (263), and when he refuses to believe that his son's infection is already fatal, Bazarov replies: "Sure! It's been over four hours." (264)

Finally, we may note that four characters die, thereby disrupting marriages or love relationships: Nikolai Petrovich's first wife, Odintsova's first husband, Princess R., and Bazarov. Yet the novel ends with four marriages: Arkadi's, his father's, Odintsova's, and Piotr's.

Partly in consequences of its fourfold orientation, *Fathers and Sons* possesses a pleasingly balanced structure that extends even to minor details. In contrast to some of the characters' verbal confrontations, the setting, action, and narration are harmonious without seeming stylized. Indeed, a major satisfaction for the reader of Turgenev's novel is that art unobtrusively orders life.

Notes

1. David Lowe, *Turgenev's Fathers and Sons* (Ann Arbor, 1983), p. 15.

2. Richard Freeborn, "The Structure of *Fathers and Sons*," in: Ralph E. Matlaw, ed., *Fathers and Sons* (Norton Critical Edition, New York, 1966), p. 292.

3. Virginia M. Burns, "The Structure of the Plot in *Otcy i deti*," *Russian Literature*, No. 6, 1974 (The Hague), pp. 40–1. She sees the novel as having five sections (p. 39).

4. Freeborn, p. 293.

One could object that this neglects Pavel-Princess R., but their love story is told in a flashback, as is that of Nikolai and Arkadi's mother. The words "involving Arkadi" could be added to Freeborn's third love story, adding symmetry to his format.

5. Lowe, p. 106.

6. Charles A. Moser, *Ivan Turgenev* (New York, 1972), pp. 26–7. Lowe develops this idea at some length (pp. 38–44).

7. Joel Blair, "The Architecture of Turgenev's *Fathers and Sons*," *Modern Fiction Studies*, Vol. XIX, No. 4 (1973–74), p. 559.

8. Lowe, p. 72.

9. Blair, p. 556.

10. Lowe, p. 76.

11. *Ibid.*, p. 53.

12. Ralph E. Matlaw's revised version of Constance Garnett's translation in the Norton Critical Edition (New York, 1966), p. 87; Rosemary Edmonds' translation in the Penguin Classics Edition (Baltimore, 1970), p. 131.

13. However, just before Bazarov's fatal infection, Turgenev somewhat abruptly tells

us that the "self-assured" Bazarov, who had boasted of how he could talk with the peasants, was nevertheless "something of a buffoon in their eyes" (262).

14. Turgenev adds a nice touch by having Arkadi himself use the word *pustyaki* (130) while expressing to his father an opinion presumably acquired from Bazarov but before we learn that the latter habitually used the word in declaring his opinions to Arkadi.

15. Lowe, pp. 80, 81.

16. *Ibid.*, p. 52.

17. Matlaw, p. 11; Edmonds, p. 28.

18. Lowe, p. 19.

19. Mitya cuts four teeth (153); Arkadi tastes four kinds of preserves (211).

11

"The Singers": A Disarming Victory

D. S. Mirsky has declared that "The Singers," one of Turgenev's *Sportsman's Sketches*, "may claim to be his crowning achievement and the quintessence of all the most characteristic qualities of his art."[1] The story is indeed an awesome gem, with some deeply moving, poetic effects. Deceptively simple, it contains colloquial words and phrases that are difficult to render in English. There are five approximately equal parts: 1) the introduction, which whets the reader's curiosity as the narrator learns of the wager and imminent singing contest; 2) a description of the two contestants; 3) a digressive history of some of the characters, increasing the suspense and eventually enriching their reactions to the singing; 4) the contest itself; and 5) its aftermath, which has been considered anticlimactic but serves a remarkable dual function. We shall examine "The Singers" in detail, seeking to discover reasons for its artistic success.

In the opening sentence (1:178), we learn that the village of Kolotovka belonged to a female landowner nicknamed *Stryganikha* because of her "bold and spirited disposition" (*likhoj i bojkij nrav*). *Stryganikha* has been rendered "the Dockmaned Filly" and "Mistress Trouncer" in English translations.[2] Especially if one knows that the author himself was repelled by his mother's cruelty to her serfs, Mistress Trouncer's "bold and spirited disposition" may seem somewhat euphemistic. The suggestive interplay of "Trouncer" and "Kolotovka" (*kolotit'* means to strike or pound; colloquially, to thrash or drub) is lost in English, though the word Kolotovka appears several times at the beginning of the story and also at the end, when a peasant boy is threatened with "a good hiding!"[3]

Also in the opening sentence, we learn that Mistress Trouncer's village of Kolotovka was "cleft by a terrible ravine." "Cleft" (*rassechyonnogo*) features the root *sech'* ("to cut, to flog"), as does the "good hiding" (*vysech'*). When the narrator enters a pub "at the very head" of this ravine, he sees the two singing contestants. Yashka the Turk is a frail young man with sunken cheeks. His hands shake as in a "fever" (this word appears three times in one sentence), and he seems to have "an impressionable, passionate nature" (182). His competitor, a tradesman, is shorter and heavy-set. He looks around "boldly" (*bojko*), talking in a carefree manner. Our narrator sums him up later (186) as shrewd and "bold" (*bojkim*), and his singing elicits the cry *Likho!* (187), echoing Mistress Trouncer's "bold, spirited" disposition.

When it is time to start the contest, the tradesman declares "coldbloodedly and with a self-assured smile" that he is ready. "I'm ready too," Yashka says "with agitation." In a third contrast, the tradesman "clears his throat" at the command to begin, whereas Yashka "shudders."

This command is uttered by the Wild Gentleman, a powerful authority among those present. As his name could suggest, the man is a combination of near ferocity and quiet contemplation. He is likened to an almost motionless bull, and Turgenev places his portrait between the introductory descriptions of Yashka and the tradesman, somewhat like a referee between two fighters.

The Wild Gentleman, we are told, avoids wine and women, but he passionately loves singing (186). Asked who is to begin, he decides to have the contestants draw lots—but not before Featherbrain, a tipsy and talkative peasant, babbles out his opinion that the tradesman should go first. Deferring to the Wild Gentleman, Featherbrain holds out his cap, into which the competitors throw similar but identifiable coins. Another peasant shakes the cap, and a dead silence falls upon the pub. The two coins "faintly jingle" as they "strike against each other"—an effective prelude to the singing contest.

When the tradesman's coin is selected, Featherbrain exults: "What did I say," he exclaims, "What did I tell you." This is paralleled by his confident reaction to the tradesman's singing. "You've won!" he tells the tradesman, "the beer is yours!" Featherbrain even echoes his earlier assertion with "I'm telling you"—although this time, of course, he will turn out to be quite wrong.

As we have seen, Turgenev carefully contrasted the frail, feverish Yashka with the bold, carefree tradesman. However, Yashka's feverishness included a passionate sensitivity, whereas the tradesman's boldness contained a cold-blooded self-assurance. Turgenev employed a similar strategy to depict the contest itself. As the tradesman begins: "His voice was quite pleasant and sweet though somewhat husky . . ." (187) He artfully "played" with his voice, which "poured forth and overflowed downwards," returning to stretch out the high notes "with a special effort." He "would grow silent" and then, suddenly, pick up the previous tune "with a kind of devil-may-care, arrogant daring." In each of these descriptions, the initially pleasant effect is slightly undermined: sweetness by huskiness; artfulness by effort; daring by arrogance. Our initial impressions of the tradesman are subtly reinforced. Finally, his masterful singing causes the stern Wild Gentleman to smile; Featherbrain and others become ecstatic. The Wild Gentleman's face has "softened somewhat," but his expression remains "disdainful."

When it is Yashka's turn, he moves his hand to his throat. Told not to lose heart, he covers his face with his hand; when he removes it, his face is as "pale as a dead man's." The first sound of Yashka's voice is "weak and uneven." It then becomes "quavering, ringing" and "trembling," like a plucked string. A "mournful song" begins "to flow." His voice sounds "broken," and it has a "slightly cracked," even "sickly" ring. But in his voice, we are told, "there was genuine, deep passion, and youth, and strength, and sweetness, and some kind of enticingly carefree sorrow." With Yashka, the descriptive technique is even more extreme: his voice must overcome a long series of unpromising qualities to assert its youthfulness, sweetness and strength. These positive qualities are reinforced by Yashka's "genuine, deep passion," yet persuasively qualified by the "enticingly carefree sorrow." However, this sorrow is immediately associated with the "Russian soul" and the sounding of "Russian strings," so that even when Yashka's voice seems almost disappointingly to "break" or "snap" at the end, it re-evokes the earlier "plucked" and "Russian" string comparisons.

Victory, it seems, would be Yashka's even if Turgenev had not also employed a characteristic descriptive technique: likening melodious sound to flowing water. A few examples may be helpful. In *Fathers and Sons*, as Arkadi contemplates the countryside: "everywhere in endless, ringing streams the larks poured forth" (3:132). English translations render the idiomatic *zalivalis'* ("poured forth") as "poured out" and "flooded," in each case adding references to the singing itself not specifically present in the Russian: "trills" and "trilling music."[4] (The verb *zalivat'sya* means "to be flooded" and "to pour," but also "to break into" or "to burst into," as, for example, tears or song.) Early in "Living Relics," we are told, of some larks: "They must have carried away dewdrops on their wings, and their songs seemed drenched in dew." (1:276) Then the crippled peasant Lukerya recalls being captivated by a nightingale's song: "He kept pouring, pouring forth." (*Zalivaetsya on, zalivaetsya*.) Finally, Lukerya herself touchingly attempts to sing: "she wanted so much to pour out [*vylit'*] her entire soul."

In "The Singers," the tradesman's voice "pours forth and overflows" (*zalivalsya i perelivalsya*) as he begins. Yashka's singing "begins to flow" (*polilas'*) somewhat later, but then "grows, overflows" (*rosla, razlivalas'*), whereupon the narrator recalls seeing at low tide (*otliva*) a large white seagull standing motionless on the seashore, "holding up its silky breast to the scarlet radiance of the sunset." Hearing Yashka's singing, he remembers that seagull, "spreading out its long wings to meet the familiar sea, to meet the deep-red sun." Yashka sings, oblivious of everyone, "yet visibly borne up, like a strong swimmer by the waves, by our silent, passionate sympathy." Tears well up in the narrator's eyes; the pub-keeper's wife is weeping. Yashka, seeing her, "pours out" (*zalilsya*) "still more ringingly, still more sweetly than before." And: "A heavy teardrop rolled slowly down the iron face of the Wild Gentleman. . ."

Whereas the tradesman's voice "flows" only early in his singing, Yashka's voice begins to flow later. Both his singing and its effect are then depicted by a variety of pouring, floating, and flooding water images. The seagull that stands motionless at low tide aptly suggests Yashka and his flowing singing. Both are delicately vulnerable: the bird, holding up its silky breast, and Yashka, touching his throat with his hand. The white bird is tinged by the sun's red glow; Yashka's face, pale as a dead man's when he began, is entirely "transformed" by the glow of victory, and "his eyes shine with happiness" (190). And whereas Yashka's singing touches Russian heartstrings, the seagull spreads its wings "to meet the familiar sea."[5]

Marianne Moore has proposed that: "Poetry is an unintelligible unmistakable vernacular like the language of the animals—a system of communication whereby a fox with a turkey too heavy for it to carry, reappears shortly with another fox to share the booty." This seems to me successful because poetry, like the appearance of the second fox, is both magical and surprising. In "The Singers," Turgenev's use of the vulnerable sunset gull to depict Yashka singing creates—with its unexpectedly rich suggestiveness—a similarly magical surprise. More than any other image in the story, it helps to promote Yashka's (and the author's) disarming victory.

The ending of the story unexpectedly reinforces our memory of the contest. The narrator avoids Yashka's celebration in the pub because, as he puts it, "I was afraid of spoiling my impression." (191) He withdraws to lie down on some hay, whereupon: "Yashka's irresistible voice rang in my ears for a long time." The narrator falls asleep; when he awakens, he notes that "the sunset had died away long ago." This parallels the change within the pub—from Yashka's "sunset seagull" singing to his, and the others', drunken carousing. It also anticipates the replacement of voices in the narrator's consciousness: as if in grotesque imitation of the singing contest, two boys yell back and forth across the night. The reference to a "good hiding," as we have noted, echoes the story's opening emphasis; at the end, with the voice of one boy shrilly ringing in the night air, we are returned to the harsh world of "Kolotovka," yet also moved to recall Yashka's delicately beautiful singing and its "enticingly carefree sorrow." Thus does coarse cruelty frame magical, sorrowful beauty.

Notes

1. D. S. Mirsky, *A History of Russian Literature from its Beginnings to 1900* (New York, 1958), p. 199.

2. Ivan Turgenev, *The Hunting Sketches*, Trans. Bernard Guilbert Guerney (New York, 1962), p. 236 and Ivan Turgenev, *First Love and Other Tales*, Trans. David Magarshack (New York, 1968), p. 1, respectively.

3. This is Magarshack's rendering of *vysech'*; Guerney has "beat the daylights out of you!"

4. Ivan Turgenev, *Fathers and Sons*, Trans. Rosemary Edmonds (Baltimore, 1970), p. 25 and Trans. and ed. Ralph E. Matlaw (New York, 1966), p. 9, respectively.

5. This is a literal and perhaps understated translation; Guerney has: "in greeting to the sea it knew so well." (p. 252.)

12

Suggestive Imagery in *Fathers and Sons*

Upon learning that Arkadi plans to marry Katya, Bazarov tells him: "So you've decided to build yourself a nest?" (3:259) Shortly thereafter, Bazarov points to a pair of jackdaws sitting side by side. The jackdaw, he declares, is a "most respected, family" bird. "An example for you!" Finally, on his deathbed, Bazarov refers to Arkadi as "a little bird," declaring that he has "joined the jackdaws now" (266). *Fathers and Sons* contains numerous other such images, but some are by no means so explicit. Let us first consider some relatively simple examples.

Bazarov is repeatedly associated with his frog-dissecting, and his death results from performing a post-mortem examination. "You and I *are* those same frogs," he had told some peasant boys (136). In the flirtation scene, Bazarov says that he wishes to have a rose from Fenechka (232); not long before this, her beauty was said to be entering an epoch likened to the blooming of "summer roses" (230). When Bazarov first visits Madame Odintsova, he asks for a drink of vodka (182); on his second visit, he asks for kvass (251). The two drinks suggestively precede his conduct: amorously intoxicated during the first visit, and humbly apologetic later. Just before his death, Bazarov tells Odintsova: "Fell under a wheel." (270) These words must be held in mind to appreciate fully his statement, a little later: "The worm is half-crushed, but it's still puffing up." Finally, even though six months are said to have passed since Bazarov's death, most readers will probably detect its reflection in the "bloody" sunset that fades early in the last chapter (272). As we shall see, numerous suggestive images in *Fathers and Sons* are taken from the realm of nature; several involve birds; and many are anticipatory.

In Chapter One, Nikolai Petrovich looks at the posting-station steps:

> A large, gaudy chicken was strutting sedately along them, firmly tapping his big yellow feet; a bespattered cat regarded him hostilely, leaning affectedly up against the railing. (127)

As David Lowe has observed, this passage suggests in miniature the drama about to be played out between "the gaudy, self-important Pavel and the hostile, occasionally mud-bespattered Bazarov."[1] Indeed, when Pavel Petrovich announces Bazarov's arrival the next morning (140), Bazarov's clothes are "bespattered" (*zapachkany*)—the same word used for the "bespattered" cat. Moreover, the sedate Pavel Petrovich "taps his fingernails" on the table (134) while asking about Bazarov, thus echoing the strutting chicken's "claw-tapping."

In the same paragraph containing the chicken and cat, we are told:

> A fat, blue-grey pigeon flew onto the road and hurriedly went to drink at a puddle beside the well.

The fat, blue-grey pigeon may be associated with Nikolai Petrovich, who, we have just learned, is now "entirely grey" and "a little chubby." Like the pigeon, he has come to the road to be refreshed (by meeting his son), and he begins watching the pigeon just as his son arrives. The image of a fat pigeon is particularly apt for Nikolai Petrovich because of his softness and weakness: "I am a soft, weak person," he admits (148).

After this admission, Nikolai Petrovich adds that his brother has "the eye of an eagle." Combining the images, we have: Arkadi and Katya—nesting jackdaws; Nikolai Petrovich—a fat, blue-grey pigeon; Pavel Petrovich—a strutting chicken with an eagle eye.

After Bazarov contracts his fatal infection, the house becomes quiet except for a "loud-mouthed cock" who is taken away, "long unable to understand why he was being treated in that manner" (265). The personified bird's confusion immediately precedes Bazarov's confused delirium, wherein he sees himself as a "black grouse," surrounded by "red dogs" (266). The red dogs derive from the "ominous red spots" on Bazarov's arm (265) that he has just shown to his father as evidence of his fatal infection; in Bazarov's delirium, his father makes the red dogs "point" at the black grouse. He then asks his father to send for Odintsova, adding: "I'll go back to my dogs now." He says this just after his declaration that Arkadi has "joined the jackdaws now"—thus linking his own "black grouse" image with the "jackdaw" description of Arkadi.

In Fenechka's room there hangs a "cage with a short-tailed siskin" (149). The bird "ceaselessly chirps and hops," while the cage "ceaselessly swings and shakes." This parallels the nervous, uneasy attitude of the peasant girl herself, who seems both "ashamed" to be with the gentlemen Kirsanovs and yet also to feel that it was her "right" (140). When Pavel Petrovich tickles Fenechka's baby (by Nikolai Petrovich) with his long fingernail, the baby stares at the siskin and laughs (149).

A brief parallel can be drawn between Sitnikov and Dunyasha: both revere Bazarov, who generally ignores them, and each is likened to a "female quail." This occurs quite naturally in Russian expressions of rapid movement (155, 201), but it aptly reflects, in both contexts, their flighty reverence for Bazarov. At the Governor's ball, Kukshina has a "bird of paradise" in her hair (175)—an appropriate suggestion of her affectations. In addition to the "loud-mouthed cock" and "black grouse" images associated with Bazarov, he is called a "falcon" (who can fly wherever he wants) by his mother (224). She is using a natural Russian expression, but it effectively reflects Bazarov's strong independence.

In his correspondence, Turgenev repeatedly referred to Bazarov as a "wolf,"[2] and Bazarov's expression is "almost bestial" (199) when he confesses his "insane" love to Odintsova. As Katya tells Arkadi, Bazarov is "predatory," whereas they are "tame" (247). Katya declares that she has helped to "remake" Arkadi (as his natural, tame self), and he later acknowledges this (255). His "remaking" is associated with Fifi, the well-behaved dog in a light-blue collar with whom Katya first appears (183). Arkadi covers up his inability to draw out Katya in conversation by calling Fifi over and petting her (186). Later, we see Katya and Arkadi in the garden with Fifi on the ground beside them (246). It is then that she calls Arkadi and herself "tame." Finally, Katya tickles Fifi's ears with the tip of her parasol and decides that Arkadi will soon be at her feet (250). Much as the image of a nervous, caged bird suggested Fenechka's difficult position at the Kirsanovs', so the obedient, collared dog suggests the "remaking" of Arkadi from "predatory" posturing to his "tame" domestic self.

When Arkadi does at last declare his love, he does so in a Greek portico where a statue of Silence has been removed (257). We learn this at the beginning of the proposal scene (254). The removal of Silence can also be associated with Bazarov's "strange conversation" with Odintsova (257), which interrupts Arkadi's declaration of his feelings to Katya.[3] In this conversation, Odintsova calls Bazarov "good," which he likens to "placing a wreath of flowers on the head of a corpse" (257). In context, he refers to her rejecting and then praising him, but the image also anticipates the flowers that speak of "indifferent" nature above his corpse in the last sentence of the novel.

Nature serves as a moral touchstone in Turgenev's works,[4] and in *Fathers and Sons* the characters who respond to the beauty of nature (Arkadi, his father, Katya, and, in his amusing way, Bazarov's father) are implicitly differentiated from those who do not (Pavel Petrovich, Odintsova, and Bazarov). Those who like nature are generally positive characters, and they generally fare better at the end. Bazarov, however, is a special case.

There is, as Odintsova suggests, much that is "good" in Bazarov, and we have Turgenev's own claim that he wanted the reader "to love Bazarov with all his coarseness."[5] Yet Bazarov is "quite indifferent" to nature (190), considering it "not a temple but a workshop" (154). He scorns Arkadi's observation that the falling motion of a sad, dead leaf oddly resembles the flight of a joyous, live butterfly (219)[6]—preferring, instead, to praise the efforts of an ant, dragging away a half-dead fly without a trace of the "compassion' felt by "self-destructive" human beings (217).

Like Arkadi, Bazarov is acting out an unnatural and somewhat unbecoming role; unfortunately, however, he is much better at it, and he has no one, like Katya, to "remake" him. Just before he advises Arkadi to be the "family" bird that he has been all along, Bazarov refers to himself as a "flying fish" (258). He says this to Odintsova, who has just asked him to remain with her. Flying fish, he explains, can only remain in the air so long: "and so permit me to flop down into my element." The self-contradiction is subtle but revealing: flying fish move naturally in two elements, and in negating the "air," Bazarov is denying himself a vital part of life.

Remaining at the Kirsanovs' after Arkadi's departure, Bazarov refrains from arguing with Pavel Petrovich; but their former hostility, as evidenced by one brief conversation, lurks beneath the surface. This leads to a description of what Pavel once saw in Bazarov's microscope:

> . . . a transparent infusoria was swallowing a green speck of dust, busily chewing it with some kind of very agile little fists that were located in its throat. (229)

The passage resists translation, but it suggests energetic predatoriness and perhaps even hostility. The word *kulachkami* ("little fists") is used in idioms for physical combat; it can also mean "cams" in modern technology.

Ralph Matlaw has: "two very rapid sort [*sic*] of clappers."[7] Rosemary Edmonds has: "two very adroit fist-like organs."[8] This microscope episode—involving the two antagonists, juxtaposed with their argument, and related to "fighting"—suggestively prefigures the duel itself.

Having accepted Pavel Petrovich's challenge, Bazarov concludes that he had no choice: Pavel would have "struck" him, and he "would have had to strangle him like a kitten" (236). With this thought in mind, Bazarov returns to his microscope. As in the previous episode, there is a destructive emphasis upon the throat. However, it is also the coldly matter-of-fact tone ("busily chewing it," "strangle him like a kitten") that links these suggestive details with the impending duel.

Indeed, the above "fist" and "throat" connections may seem, in their suggestiveness, akin to the strange logic of dreams. Bazarov himself evinces such logic when he is delirious (the "red dogs" for the "red spots")—or actually dreaming. The night before the duel, he dreams the following:

> Odintsova was whirling before him; now she was his mother; behind her walked a small cat with little black whiskers, and the cat was Fenechka; then Pavel Petrovich appeared to him as a large forest, with which he had yet to fight. (236–7)

This dream, with its matter-of-fact impossibilities, takes us through the novel. Bazarov's "whirling" passion for Odintsova is followed by his return to his parents and later, by his flirting with Fenechka (her "little black whiskers" are a dream distortion of the kiss), witnessed by Pavel Petrovich, who then proposes the duel. The "forest, with which he had yet to fight" appears at the end of the novel, as James Justus has observed.[9] Bazarov, on his deathbed, attempts to articulate what is useful and "needed." This gives way to delirious confusion and the words: "There's a forest there." (271)

It should be noted that Bazarov's delirium fulfills the prophetic ending of his dream despite his moribund efforts to retain rational control. The nihilist's rational mind, seeking out what is useful and "needed," distrusts the undisciplined realms of delirium and dreams. Thus Bazarov, clenching his fists, insists that he must not become delirious (267)—and he forbids Arkadi to look at his "stupid expression" while he sleeps (217). Yet Bazarov may well have realized, at death, that there are mysterious truths beyond the reach of the rational mind: the "realized" forest image can be traced, in part, to his own previously articulated ideas.

Bazarov, we may recall, declared to Odintsova that "people are like trees in a forest" (184). In his coldly analytical view, there is no need to study each individual tree—just as "one human example is sufficient to judge all the others." Shortly thereafter, we are told that in Bazarov's conversations with Odintsova:

> . . . he expressed still more strongly his indifferent contempt for everything romantic; but when he was alone, he would recognize with indignation the romantic in himself. Then he would go off to the forest and walk through it with long strides, breaking the small branches before him and cursing under his breath both her and himself . . . (190)

As Bazarov struggles against succumbing to his inner feelings, he significantly vents his frustration upon the trees of the forest. Translators have reduced the revealing tension of "indifferent contempt," thus muting Turgenev's suggestion that Bazarov is at odds with his true self.[10]

Later, Bazarov admits to Arkadi that in his childhood, a certain aspen tree had seemed to possess talismanic powers, but now that he has grown up, "the talisman does not work" (215–6). Only at Bazarov's death, when the forest image becomes "realized" through irrational truth, is the talismanic power of his childhood perhaps reactivated. In other terms, the "flying fish" may have realized that it was wrong to negate the "air." Bazarov, we can infer, has found in his inexorable return to Nature the "temple" he had previously denied: the flowers on his grave ". . . speak not only of eternal peace and the great peace of 'indifferent' nature; they speak also of eternal reconciliation and life without end."

Bazarov's encounter with the forest ("with which he had yet to fight") leads, finally, to the enlightened attainment of a "great peace." In fact, the novel's suggestive imagery is continuously in harmony with the realms of nature, delirium, and dreams. The "fight" becomes an acceptance. Both Arkadi's and his father's sentimental views are, in the end, ironically supported by the moribund insight of the cynical Bazarov, whose return to the talismanic power of his childhood trees can be seen as a peaceful re-evaluation.

Notes

1. David Lowe, *Turgenev's Fathers and Sons* (Ann Arbor, 1983), p. 52. In the Norton Critical Edition of the novel, Ralph E. Matlaw's translation has the cat bestowing his hostile look upon Nikolai Petrovich rather than upon the chicken. (New York, 1966, p. 3.)

2. See Ralph E. Matlaw, Trans. and ed., *Fathers and Sons* (New York, 1966), pp. 186, 188.

3. Alexander Fischler, who discusses this episode in detail, has observed that the "traditional message" of Arkadi's and Katya's "need for commitment and true love" comes through the portico of Silence. See his "The Garden Motif and the Structure of Turgenev's *Fathers and Sons,*" *Novel,* Vol. 9, No. 3 (Spring 1976), pp. 252–4.

4. See Lowe, p. 107.

5. Matlaw, p. 186.

6. Pierre Hart, who notes that Bazarov's "workshop" description of nature comes from Chernyshevsky, sees Arkadi's poetic pleasure in the falling leaf as "precipitating the final round" in the two friends' quarrel. ("Nature as the Norm in *Otcy i deti,*" *Russian Language Journal,* Vol. XXXI, No. 110, Fall 1977, pp. 56, 58, 61.)

7. Matlaw, p. 116.

8. Ivan Turgenev, *Fathers and Sons,* Trans. Rosemary Edmonds (Baltimore, 1970), p. 170.

9. James H. Justus, *"Fathers and Sons:* The Novel as Idyll," in: Matlaw, Trans. and ed., *Fathers and Sons,* p. 311.

10. Matlaw has "calm contempt" (p. 73); Edmonds, "quiet scorn" (p. 112). The Russian is *ravnodushnoe prezrenie* (190).

13

Gogol's Phonetic Emphasis

Readers of Nikolai Gogol's works encounter furniture that proclaims "I am Sobakevich!", a choir of doors and a choir of dogs (the Tovstogubs' and Korobochka's)—one of the doors sings out: "Dear friends, I am freezing!"—and a rooster who seems to say "greetings and salutations" to Chichikov. In "The Carriage," a man who wishes to kiss his wife's neck in bed makes "a low mooing sound like a calf emits when seeking the teats of its mother." And in "Viy," a man produces "such deep laughter as if two bulls, each facing the other, bellowed simultaneously."

Gogol's uncanny imagination often expressed itself phonetically. He worked with silence and sound the way a painter uses shadows and highlights. Both add a dimension; both are surprisingly vivid or eloquent. Gogol's characters assume soundless, frozen poses. They silently spy upon one another. And Gogolian mouths produce a variety of unusual noises, some of which have a relevance well beyond their immediate context.

In *Dead Souls*, Chichikov promises to bring the Manilovs' son a drum, a "grand" one: "toorrr . . . roo . . . tra-ta-ta, ta-ta-ta . . . farewell, dear boy, farewell!" (6:38) This parallels Chichikov's charming of the boy's parents. He has just declared that if he and the Manilovs lived together it would be "a paradisiacal life"—whereupon he also said "farewell" to each of them. A child's drum is round, colorful, and hollow; it is full of air and makes impressive sounds. So is Chichikov himself: he is plump, colorfully clothed, and has impressed an inn servant by his trumpet-like nose blowing. Carl Proffer has called Chichikov "a little burst of irritating hot air born into the world through a nose which is like a horn."[1] The imaginary drum (quite literally, one suspects, a hollow promise) may even be associated with Chichikov's dealings in dead souls throughout the novel. These transactions also involve vivid but phantom objects, leading ultimately to the hero's hasty "farewell."

Early in *The Inspector General,* we learn that the doctor Christian Ivanovich cannot communicate with his patients because he does not know a word of Russian (4:13). At this point, the man "produces a sound partially resembling the letter *i* and somewhat like the letter *e*." To a Russian ear, this phonetic hybrid suggests the man's Germanness, as Simon Karlinsky has noted.[2] And since the poor communicator is a doctor, it also reflects the town's rampant inefficiency. But what are we to think, soon after this, when Christian Ivanovich produces *"the very same sound"* (14)? This "precise" repetition of something so vague and alien is faintly humorous in a humorous context, but its relevance extends further: oddly comic duplication is central to this play. We have twin absurd marriage proposals, two series of comic bribings, the clown-like Bobchinski and Dobchinski, and of course two Inspector Generals.

Describing his "discovery" of the Inspector, Bobchinski declares that he was enlightened from above and said "Eh!" (19) Dobchinski interrupts to insist that he was the one who said "Eh!" Bobchinski argues that first, Dobchinski said it, and then he did: they both said "Eh!" Besides comically retarding their report, the repeated "eh!" sound accords with the reaction of the town's officials, who are quite literally struck dumb by the idea of the Inspector's arrival. When it is finally revealed that Khlestakov is an imposter, Dobchinski again says "eh" just before the real Inspector is announced and the final scene of mute stupefaction begins.

In Gogol's story "The Carriage," the General draws on his pipe, releases smoke, and praises his horse:

". . . the horse, poof, poof, is very respectable!"

"And have you, your excellency, poof, poof, owned her for a long time?" said Chertokutski.

"Poof, poof, poof, poo . . . poof, not so long. Only two years in all, since I got her at the stud-farm!"

"And did you obtain her already broken in or did you have her broken in here?"

"Poof, poof, poo, poo, poo . . . oo . . . oo . . . f, here,"—having said that, the General completely disappeared in smoke (3:181)

The General's "poofing"[3] increasingly encroaches upon his spoken words, much as the smoke increasingly obscures his body. The printed effect reinforces the depicted one. Moreover, this episode promotes a curious symmetry. Here, as the General praises his horse, smoke gradually hides him from Chertokutski's view. At the climax of the story, it is the General who discovers Chertokutski, hiding in his own much-praised carriage, whereupon we read that he "covered up Chertokutski again" with the carriage rug and departed.

In *Dead Souls*, Chichikov's relationship with each of the five landowners with whom he bargains has its own phonetic emphasis. With Sobakevich, it is the sound "oo" in Russian (*u*). When Chichikov arrives, bear-like Sobakevich invites him in with a gruff *"Proshú!"* (6:94) He then indicates a chair and booms out *"Proshu!"* once again. Sobakevich's wife Feodulia also greets Chichikov with *"Proshu!"*

Having invited his guest to eat (with yet another *"Proshu!"*), Sobakevich so strongly disparages the Governor's food that Feodulia exclaims *"Fu!"* Sobakevich declares that so-called enlightenment is—*"fuk!"* After dinner, as they bargain about dead souls, Chichikov says that this subject is simply *"fufu"* (104). Finally, discovering the name of a female serf, Chichikov exclaims *"Fu"* (137), concluding that Sobakevich has "swindled" him (*nadúl*).

These "oo" sounds are reinforced by numerous others. For example, Feodúlia is termed the "spouse" (*suprúga*) of Sobakevich as she exclaims *"Fu!"* and the bargaining over dead souls includes: *Kak mukhi mrut . . . po stu rublej za shtuku! . . . takuyu summu!* And when the bargaining reaches an uneasy impasse, a portrait on the wall is said to stare intently at "this purchase" (*ètu pokupku*).

At the Manilovs', the phonetic emphasis is upon "oh," or perhaps more precisely, "awe" in Russian (*o*). When Chichikov arrives, he praises the town and its officials, using the word "very" (*óchen'*) again and again (27–8). Both he and Manilov (who may be considered a sort of dreamy zero) then frequently begin their sentences with *"O,"* or *"O!"* This tends to amplify their wonder-stricken awe as they praise each other. For example, both exclaim *"O"* when they agree upon the value of their friendship (29)—and again when they dream of living together in the future (37). And when Chichikov explains the nature of his commerce, Manilov's mouth (*rot*) drops open, whereupon he remains "with gaping mouth for several minutes." The bargaining itself also contains the *"o"* emphasis, for instance, Manilov's statement that many serfs have died: ". . . *óchen' mnógie umirali! Tóchno, óchen' mnógie."* (33) And as Manilov (with an *"O!"*) assures

Chichikov that he is content with the deal, it is termed a "negotiation" (*negótsiya*) three times.

Nozdryov is an impulsive, explosive rogue, bursting with health. He favors the sound "bah" (*ba*), using words like *baly* ("balls"), *baby* ("broads"), and, especially often, *bank* and its diminutive *banchik* in reference to his passion for gambling. Recognizing Chichikov at the inn, Nozdryov exclaims: *"Ba, ba, ba! Kakimi sud'bami?"* (64) The Russian interjection *ba* expresses surprise upon recognizing someone. Here, it is significantly echoed by *sud'bámi* ("fates," suggesting "What brings you here?"): Nozdryov soon insists that "fate" has brought him and Chichikov together (*"sud'bá svela"*)—and since his blabbing later exposes Chichikov's dealings in dead souls, Nozdryov can be considered a fateful force working against him.[4] Indeed, Chichikov barely escapes from Nozdryov's estate without a beating.

Just prior to his *"Ba, ba, ba!"* exclamation, Nozdryov is described as a man with white "teeth" (*zubámi*) and black "sideburns" (*bakenbárdami*). Numerous other references to his *bakenbardy*, his dogs (*sobáki*), and his gambling (*bank, bánchik, bánku*) reinforce the "bah" emphasis. Nozdryov even suggests both gambling and dog-purchasing to thwart Chichikov's attempts to buy dead souls, and when he had first approached Nozdryov, Chichikov's desire was termed a "request" (*pros'ba*) three times (77). As with Sobakevich and Manilov, even the term applied to the deal reflects the phonetic emphasis.

Korobochka's pronouncements feature the sound "okh." When Chichikov wonders if some of her serfs have died, she answers *"Okh"* (50): eighteen people. He then points out that she is still paying taxes for the dead. *"Okh,"* she exclaims (52): don't speak about that! Finally, Chichikov becomes so frustrated that he tells Korobochka to go to the devil. *"Okh,"* she replies (54): don't mention him, God be with him!

Korobochka's frightened, woeful *"okh"*s suit her personality: she is introduced as the kind of female landowner who "laments" about "bad harvests" and "losses" (45). Her first complaint to Chichikov occurs when he asks how she has slept. "Badly" (*Plókho*), she answers. She also laments that "the times are bad" (*plókhi*), and the harvest is bad too (*plokh*). Like Manilov's *"O"*s, Korobochka's *"okh"*s require a rounding of the mouth. It thus seems appropriate that Korobochka, like Manilov, hesitates with mouth agape during the negotiations (53)—wondering if dead souls might somehow be useful around the house.

In contrast to Korobochka's mournful "okh," we have Plyushkin's joyful "akh!" This sound aptly suggests the miser's delight when Chichikov offers to pay the taxes on the (dead) serfs:

> "Akh, my dear fellow! Akh, my benefactor!" Plyushkin cried out, not noticing in his joy that tobacco was emerging from his nose in an exceedingly unpicturesque manner, rather like dense coffee; and the flaps of his robe, swinging open, revealed garments not exceedingly decent for inspection. (123)

Throughout this passage, Plyushkin's two *"akh"*s are reinforced by stressed "ah" sounds, for example, *ne zamecháya ot rádosti* ("not noticing in his joy"). Others include "my dear fellow!" (*bátyushka!*), two uses of "exceedingly" (*ves'má*), "tobacco" (*tobák*), and "robe" (*khaláta*). Plyushkin continues to express his joy with "Akh, my God! Akh, my prelates! . . ." and, when the transaction nears finalization: "Akh, *bátyushki!*" *(126)*

The phonetic emphasis of Chichikov's five dealings may be summarized as follows: Sobakevich ("oo"), Manilov ("o" or "awe"), Nozdryov ("bah"), Korobochka ("okh"), and Plyushkin ("akh"). In all five cases, the landowners themselves reinforce the emphasis with short exclamations. Moreover, the chameleon-like Chichikov tends to blend in with the pattern. He gives Manilov an "O" for an "O," Nozdryov, "pros'ba"s for his "sud'ba"s, and even doubles the Sobakevichs' "fu" and "fuk" as "fufu."

As one could expect, the phonetic emphasis in "Viy" is upon the sound "vee" (*vi*)—most frequently, in uses of "to see" (*vídet'*). The stressed "vee" sound thus reflects the hero Homa's eerie fright at what he "sees." During the old woman's nocturnal ride upon his back (2:186), a long series of "he saw . . . he saw" (*on vídel . . . on vídel*) culminates in: "Does he see this, or does he not see?" (*Vidit li on èto, ili ne vidit?*) And when Homa reads over the girl's body in church: ". . . he saw that the corpse was trying to catch him, but not where he was standing; one could see that it could not see him." (210) The three references to sight (*uvidel, vidno, videt'*) are reinforced by the word "catch" (*lovíl*). The old woman also tried to catch (*lovila*) Homa (185) just before riding on his back.

During Homa's final reading (216), the corpse's "screaming" (*vzvízgivaya*) incantations cause a "whirlwind" (*Víkhor'*), whereupon he "only sees" (*vídel tol'ko*) monstrous phenomena. "Bring in Viy! Go get Viy!" screams the corpse (*Privedite Víya! stupajte za Víem!*). Homa "sees" (*uvídel*) Viy, who says that he "cannot see" (*ne vízhu!*). The creature's eyelids are then raised, and Homa dies of fright.

As in *Dead Souls,* the phonetic emphasis of "Viy" is reinforced by brief exclamations. Lost in the dark, Homa says: "Vish', what can we do?" (182) When he asks the old woman for food, she exclaims "Vish', what you don't want!" (184) And when Homa is prevented from escaping, he thinks "Vish', devil's son!" (190)

The phonetic emphasis of "The Overcoat" involves the sound "ookh" (*ukh*). This sound appropriately reflects the discouraged resignation of the meek hero. However, it is also associated with Akaki's vulnerable inner hope and his final revenge.

Early in the story (3:143) Akaki is likened, because of his insignificance, to a common "fly" (*mukha*). Moreover, he habitually eats his supper "flies and all" (*s mukhami*). When he realizes that he must buy a new overcoat (153), Akaki falls completely "in spirit" (*dukhom*). While saving money, however, he is nourished "spiritually" (*dukhovno*) by the idea of his new coat. Thus preoccupied, he almost makes a mistake in his copying, whereupon he cries out " *'ukh!'* almost aloud" (155). This exclamation (Akaki's only one in the story) characteristically reinforces the phonetic emphasis—as does the word "aloud" (*vslukh*).

Having obtained his new coat, Akaki is said to be in the happiest state "of spirit" (*dukha*). He latter leaves a party (160) in a merry state "of spirit" (*dukha*). The imagined coat (which nourished him "spiritually") has now materialized as the sustenance of his state "of spirit." When the coat is stolen and Akaki appeals to the Important Person, he tries to collect what little "presence of spirit" (*prisútstviya dúkha*) remains (166). The Important Person indignantly asks Akaki where he got such nerve—literally, collected such "spirit" (*dukhu*). Akaki then returns home entirely "swollen" (*raspukh*) and "releases his spirit" (*ispustil dukh*).[5] Finally, as "rumors" (*slukhi*) relate the vengeance of Akaki's ghost, we learn that the Important Person had felt something akin to pity "soon after the departure of the raked-over-the-coals Akaki Akakievich" (171). "Raked-over-the-coals" (*raspechyonnogo v pukh*) creates a phonetic play between the two descriptions of moribund Akaki: *pukh, raspukh.* When the Important Person hears of Akaki's death, he remains "out of sorts" (literally, "not in spirit," *ne v dukhe*) all day; and when Akaki's ghost haunts him, he drives home "at full speed" (literally, "in all spirit," *vo ves' dukh*).

Vladimir Nabokov has suggested that Akaki Akakievich is actually a ghost disguised as a petty official, who gradually dissolves until, at the end, he seems to be a real ghost.[6] If this is so, the inner consistency of

Akaki's transformation (from disguised ghost to revealed ghost) is phonetically reflected in the transformation from ostensible *mukha* to released
dukh.

In the very different story "Ivan Fyodorovich Shponka and His Aunt,"
the hero is not unlike Akaki: meek, bullied, and sadly, humorously inar-
ticulate. Alone with the girl to whom he is expected to propose, Ivan
Fyodorovich remains silent for about fifteen minutes.

> Finally, Ivan Fyodorovich gathered his courage. "In summer there are many flies,
> Miss!" (1:305)

The girl agrees, and this is the extent of their conversation. The Russian
rendered as "gathered his courage" contains the word *dúkhom* ("spirit");
"flies" is *mukh*. With Gogolian precarious logic,[7] this "ookh" emphasis is
amplified in a series of strangely interconnected episodes. First, young
Shponka's "entire life" (285) is "influenced" when a teacher seizes him by
the ear (*úkho*). Then Storchenko *twice* tells Shponka a story (291, 297)
about how a cockroach once crawled into his ear (*úkho*). Finally, there is
Shponka's dream in which someone seizes him by the ear (*úkho*). The
someone is a wife, and later in the dream, he removes a wife from his ear
(*úkha*). The wife is thus phonetically associated with an entire-life-influ-
encing teacher and a cockroach as the "ookh" emphasis of Shponka's
fly-preempted proposal echoes grotesquely in his nightmare of marriage.

In "The Diary of a Madman," Poprishchin, lusting after the director's
daughter, interrupts himself: "Ekh, knavery!" (3:196) A few lines later,
he exclaims "Ai, ai, ai! What a voice! A canary, truly a canary!" Associated
with knavery, the "ekh" sound (*èkh*) suggests Poprishchin's guilt and
shame. Also appropriately, the "ai" sound (*aj*) suggests his excitement and
lust. The two exclamations occur in three other pairs, each of which tends
to fit this pattern.

First, an actress reminds Poprishchin of the director's daughter: "ekh,
knavery!" (199) A few lines later, we learn that "for her, ai! ai!" he
sharpened four pens at the office. Next, he imagines himself spying upon
the director's living quarters: "ekh, what rich furnishings!" (199) and upon
the daughter in her bedroom: "ai! ai! ai!" Here, the repeated *ai* immediately
echoes his conviction that her bedroom is "paradise" (*rai*). Finally, when
the director's daughter is mentioned in Madge's letter: "Ai, ai!" (202) As

he reads on, Poprishchin feels guilty ("Ekh, knavery!") but finishes the letter anyway.

"Nevsky Prospect" opens by praising this shining street and ends by describing its deceptive gleam when Satan himself lights the street lamps. At the beginning, we read: "And the women! O, Nevsky Prospect is still more pleasing to the women." At the end: "O, don't trust this Nevsky Prospect! . . . trust the women least of all."

Throughout the story, the exclamation "O" attends deceptions involving women. Advised to follow the girl who has caught his eye, Piskaryov replies: "O, how is that possible! As if she's one of those women who walk along Nevsky in the evening . . . !" (3:15–16) Disillusioned, he dreams that she has a secret which she asks him to keep: "O, I will! I will!" (26) Piskaryov then has an opium-induced vision in which she asks if she could really be a prostitute: "O! no, no!" he exclaims (29). Finally, the prostitute ridicules his proposal of marriage. "O, that was just too much!" (33) Within a few lines, the disillusioned Piskaryov has cut his throat.

The pattern continues with Pirogov. Planning to cuckold Schiller, Pirogov asks him if he can make a case for his dagger. "O, I certainly can," the unsuspecting Schiller replies (41). Then, upon catching his wife with Pirogov, Schiller exclaims: "O, I don't want to be cuckolded!" (44)

One remarkable aspect of the phonetic patterns in "Nevsky Prospect" and "The Diary of a Madman" is that each story contains an *appropriate* echo of the other. Poprishchin makes a "discovery" about women:

O, what a treacherous creature is woman! I have only now realized what a woman is. . . . Women are in love with the devil. Look at her there, aiming her lorgnette from a box in the front row. Do you think that she is watching that fat man with the star? Not at all; she is watching the devil, who is standing behind his back. (3:209)

A few lines after this, Poprishchin tells us that he went walking on "Nevsky Prospect." Turning to the end of *that* story, we find:

O, don't trust this Nevsky Prospect! . . . Do you imagine that these two fat men, who have stopped before the church that is being built, are discussing its architecture? Not at all . . . Do you think that these women . . . but trust women least of all. (3:45–6)

Introduced by exclamatory "O"s, the two passages contain other similar details: the treachery of women, the deceptiveness of the fat men, and even the phrases "Do you think" and "Not at all." Moreover, the "Nevsky" passage goes on to declare that "Satan himself" lights the street lamps to disguise the appearance of things, which corresponds to "the devil" in Poprishchin's discovery about woman's "treachery." The "O" exclamation is very unusual for Poprishchin, who, as we have seen, favors "ekh" and "ai."

Returning to "Nevsky Prospect," we find that Piskaryov, who does favor "O"s, exclaims "Ai, ai, ai, how lovely!" (3:25) in the dream that follows his disillusionment. In this dream, he desperately envisions his prostitute as pure and innocent, much as Poprishchin, in his madness, considers the director's daughter capable of loving him. Also as with Poprishchin, the repeated *ai* in Piskaryov's dream is reinforced by the word *rai* ("paradise").

The life of the heroes in "Old World Landowners" is first described as "so quiet, so quiet" (*tak tikha, tak tikha*) that one tends to forget about "the evil spirit" (2:13). Pulheria Ivanovna later says to her husband: ". . . a cat is a quiet [*tikhoe*] creature; it won't do evil to anyone." (28) She then becomes convinced that her imminent death has been signaled by her cat (30). Finally, her husband thinks that he hears the deceased Pulheria calling him on a "quiet" (*tikh*) day, whereupon he too dies. The narrator then describes the "mysterious call" of death, which occurs, he claims, during a deathly "silence" (*tishina*), a terrible silence (*tishiny*).

All these suggestions of quiet contain the sound "ee" in Russian (*i*); the last three are associated with the "mysterious call" of death. Just before *his* death, Pulheria's husband thinks that he hears his dead wife call "Afanasi Ivanovich!" (37)—and just before her death, Pulheria had called her cat: "Kis, kis!" (29) The sound "ee" thus lurks in "calls of death" relating to both landowners. Pulheria's "Kis, kis!" can be likened to Akaki's "ukh!", Homa's "vish'"s, Nozdryov's "ba"s, and so on.

In "The Nose," just prior to Kovalyov's discovery that his nose is missing, he: ". . . awoke rather early and made a 'brr . . .' with his lips—which he always did when he woke up, although he himself couldn't explain the reason." (3:52) Kovalyov then looks in the mirror and learns of his loss.

Kovalyov's allegedly enigmatic "brr" sound is actually an apt reaction to the disappearance of his nose—eerie fright and chilly nakedness. Moreover, it functions as a sort of phonetic climax: Kovalyov's "brr" is preceded by numerous references to "shaving" (*brit'*)—eleven in just over three pages—some of them even reinforced, for instance *sobralsya brit'* ("intended to shave").

We may conclude that many of Gogol's works have their own distinctive phonetic emphasis. This emphasis reverberates in important episodes and promotes an appropriate emotional atmosphere. Remarkably often, exclamatory declarations reinforce the emphasis. In *Dead Souls*, for example, Chichikov's dealings with each of the five landowners fits this pattern. In each case, moreover, the emphasis reflects the landowner's personality and informs the bargaining as well. Though far less spectacular than many of Gogol's characteristic effects, a patterned phonetic emphasis subtly enriches the magic of his art.

Notes

1. Carl R. Proffer, *The Simile and Gogol's Dead Souls* (The Hague, 1967), p. 120.

2. Simon Karlinsky, "Portrait of Gogol as a Word Glutton, with Rabelais, Sterne, and Gertrude Stein as Background Figures," *California Slavic Studies*, V (1970), p. 172.

3. Andrei Biely has quoted this "poofing" together with Chichikov's drum imitation in a series of Gogolian sound effects, but he does not discuss them. (Andrei Belyi, *Masterstvo Gogolya*, Munich, 1969, p. 169.)

4. In view of this, Gogol's statement that Nozdryov is "perhaps" destined "to play by no means the least role in our tale" (6:70) acquires a shade of archness, which it shares with the narrator's apology in Dostoevsky's *The Brothers Karamazov* for devoting so much time to the "ordinary lackey" Smerdyakov and his "hope" that Smerdyakov will "somehow on his own fit into the further development of the story." (9:129)

5. As Boris Eikhenbaum has noted: "In the general context, even this common expression sounds strange, uncommon, and almost seems like a pun—a constant phenomenon in Gogol's language." (B. M. Eikhenbaum, *"Kak sdelana 'Shinel' ' Gogolya,"* *Skvoz' litaraturu*, Leningrad, 1924, p. 193.)

6. Vladimir Nabokov, *Nikolai Gogol* (New York, 1961), pp. 143, 146.

7. See my *Through Gogol's Looking Glass: Reverse Vision, False Focus, and Precarious Logic* (New York, 1976), pp. 7–8.

14

Gogolesque Perception-Expanding Reversals in Nabokov

Vladimir Nabokov's acrobatic disclaimers may often be safely qualified, and his strenuous self-estrangement from Gogol is no exception.
Nabokov has declared: "Desperate Russian critics, trying hard to find an
Influence and to pigeonhole my own novels, have once or twice linked me
up with Gogol, but when they looked again I had untied the knots and the
box was empty."[1] And: "It is Gogol's world and as such wholly different
from Tolstoy's world, or Pushkin's, or Chekhov's or my own."[2] Both asser-
tions deceptively effect an illusion of dissimilarity far greater than that
which is in fact claimed. Also typically, they seem carefully calculated to
discourage attempts at comparing Nabokov with—and perhaps thus finding
him partly dependent upon—Gogol. When asked in 1967 if Gogol had
influenced him, Nabokov replied: "I was careful *not* to learn anything from
him. As a teacher, he is dubious and dangerous. . . . at his best, he is
incomparable and inimitable."[3] To deny being the pupil of a sometimes
inimitable writer is still not necessarily to deny natural affinity and perhaps
even influence.

Gogol and Nabokov—two very different writers—are surprisingly
alike in many ways, ranging from a fondness for depicting *poshlust*[4] to a
deep preoccupation with painting. Parallels and parodies are of course
mostly unlabeled.[5] But perhaps more important than the artistic purpose
behind Gogolisms in Nabokov is that the mechanisms of many similar
effects are nearly identical. And uniquely so. Both writers frequently con-
trive very similar "reversal effects" that conduce to a sudden, fresh view
of "reality" and, somewhat paradoxically, a simultaneous and unsettling
awareness of human perceptual limitations.

To begin with, both Gogol and Nabokov are fond of what may be termed Pandora's-box words[6]—innocent little trap doors opening into other, eerie realities. As Nabokov himself has said of Gogol, "this or that word, sometimes a mere adverb or a preposition, for instance the word 'even' or 'almost,' is inserted in such a way as to make the harmless sentence explode in a wild display of nightmare fireworks."[7] Most often, such unsettling little words serve to reverse illusion and reality, good and bad, life and death.

"Lance," a Nabokov quasi-science-fiction short story, calmly begins as follows: "The name of the planet, presuming it has already received one, is *immaterial*."[8] In *Pale Fire*, Kinbote speaks of his crown jewels and "diamond-studded crown in—*no matter*, where" (p. 195). Since these royal accouterments are presumably a madman's fabrications, and hence "non-matter," his apparently unwitting pun has an eerie ring indeed. Another pun that subtly undermines "reality" is double. While Luzhin (*The Defense*) slips off in a half-insane trance, we read that "there was something *sense*less about his ab*sence*" (p. 149).

Nabokov's punnish reversals are highly versatile. They can create a strange telepathy ("his silence irritated Martha *unspeakably*"); a teasingly disturbing feeling ("Franz felt uncomfortable to the point of *numbness*"); perversely arousing breasts ("when she bent low . . . he noticed the parting of her breasts and was *relieved* when the black silk of her bodice became *taut* again")[9]; a behind-the-scenes morality ("This girl's young sister was already earning a *decent* living as an artist's model")[10]; a typical Nabokovian irony ("This disappointed me, but *happily* his smile vanished immediately"); and even a rule uneasily proved by its exception ("As a rule, I have always been noted for my *exceptional* humorousness").[11] Nabokov's ". . . endless yawns—could not get his *fill* of them—" (*Despair*, p. 19) may be compared with Gogol's "*bursting* from hunger" in *The Inspector General* (4:27).

The word "good," however, is Nabokov's favorite such reversal word—just as "better" (*luchshe*) is Gogol's. Nabokov: "Let me dally a little, he is as *good* as destroyed"; "Without his glasses he was as *good* as blind"; "One respectable burgher, who suddenly, for no *good* reason, had dismembered a neighbor's child. . . ."[12] Gogol: "In this same village there often appeared a person, or, *better*, a devil in human form."[13] Here, the effect seems not unlike Kinbote's more subtle assertion that "present day bards, owing perhaps to *better* opportunities of aging, look like gorillas or vultures."[14]

Life and death reversals are the most far-reaching in both Nabokov and Gogol. In Gogol's *Overcoat*, Akaki's ghost threateningly reveals "a fist of a size rarely met with *even* among the living" (3:174).[15] Plyushkin, in *Dead Souls*, is described as "some kind of *gap* in humanity" (6:119), and the many hospital patients in *The Inspector General* are said to be "*getting well* like flies" (4:45). In Nabokov's *The Enchanter*, a woman who has a fatal malady in her abdomen is seen as "pregnant with her own death."[16] In Gogol's *The Sorochinsk Fair*, a peasant falls senseless to the ground and lies there "dumb and motionless" like "a terrifying *inhabitant* of a cramped coffin" (1:128). The Russian word for "inhabitant" (*zhilets*), with the same root as "life," can be seen to effect a particularly insidious life and death reversal in conjunction with "cramped coffin."

Such playful but uncanny insinuations are not mere manifestations of Gogol's famous "sad laughter." Rather, they seem more closely akin to Tyutchev's gaping "night chaos" waiting patiently beneath the bright but fragile surface of what we "perceive," or Borges's "crevices of unreason" which inform us that the "firm" architecture of the world is "false,"[17] or Biely's "thought-ark" traversing a primordial ocean of matter, or— Nabokov's numerous eerie puns.

Nabokov's life and death reversals can be relatively playful ("town life generally, that's what is boring me to death") or disturbingly humorous ("a morbid fear of pregnancy") or Gogolianly unsettling: "Horror and helpless revulsion merged in those nightmares with a certain nonterrestrial sensation, *known to those who have just died*, or have suddenly gone insane after deciphering the meaning of everything."[18]

One such reversal in *Lolita* is almost diabolically subtle. "Every blessed morning"[19] (during July in the woods at camp), we are told, "Lo would be left as sentinel, while Barbara and the boy copulated behind a bush. . . . At first, Lo had refused 'to try what it was like,' but curiosity and camaraderie prevailed, and soon she and Barbara were doing it by turns with the silent, coarse and surly but indefatigable Charlie, who had as much sex appeal as a raw carrot but sported a fascinating collection of contraceptives which he used to fish out of a third nearby lake, a considerably larger and more populous one, called Lake Climax, after the booming young factory town of that name" (p. 139). This humorous near-definition of "camaraderie" finds amusing contrast in Charlie's silent, almost devoted surliness. The "raw carrot" image, vividly suggestive in itself, gains punnish humor through its proximity to "indefatigable." Laughing perhaps at

"Lake Climax" and the explosive combination "booming young," one can easily miss the literally lethal humor of "populous." One casual reader may take it as people living nearby, or even as fish (the word *is* there); another as vaguely describing the town. Actually, of course, "populous" refers to the lake's richness in floating contraceptives, but with a sinister Gogolian twist. Since the contraceptives are doubtless used ones, the lake really is—at least in a strangely morbid sense tending to reverse life and death— partially "populous" after all.

Gogol and Nabokov both favor digressions that abruptly but subtly reverse their own descriptive direction. The result is a haunting return to the point of departure even while narrational focus seems to keep moving away. Such reversals often add a tang of uneasy humor.

Early in *Dead Souls*, we are told that the Manilovs were wont to affix to each other's lips "such a long and languid kiss that in its duration one could easily have smoked through a small straw cigar" (6:26). The descriptive technique superimposes strange images. Through a large cloud of smoke, we refocus upon that long and languid kiss, whereupon the oral pleasure of smoking uneasily haunts the Manilovs' bliss.

The return can be made from much further away. Later, we read that Plyushkin's tiny little eyes "ran out from under his bushy brows like mice, when, having poked their keen little snouts out of dark holes, ears alert and whiskers twitching, they peer out to see if a cat or prankish brat is lurking about, and suspiciously sniff the very air" (6:116). So vivid do the mice's eyes become that one almost forgets it is their bodies to which Plyushkin's eyes were initially, explicitly compared. And so convincing is Plyushkin's inferentially "suspicious" expression that few readers will notice, two pages later, when Plyushkin "became more suspicious," that the word has not been applied to him before.[20]

Such passages can be considerably longer and exceedingly complex. Early in Gogol's novel, the "black tailcoats" at the governor's party are likened to flies, which, as Nabokov has explained, ultimately twist the parodied Homeric rambling comparison into a circle by arranging themselves "here separately, there in dense clusters" just as the tailcoats had done initially (*Nikolai Gogol*, p. 79). In addition to this, the next long sentence mentions, among several humorously humanesque descriptions, that the flies "had not flown in to eat at all, but only to show themselves off, to walk back and forth" (6:14).

One would not expect Nabokov to ignore this device in his own writings. The 1966 revised edition of his autobiography contains this passage: "Now the colored pencils in action. The green one, by a mere whirl of the wrist, could be made to produce a ruffled tree, or the eddy left by a submerged crocodile."[21] Much of the tree, and especially its "ruffles," seems vividly, aptly green. But the "eddy" is more complex. Somehow hauntingly, the (greenish) invisible crocodile tends to make the (greenish) eddy it left behind even more green. Or is the submerged crocodile completely invisible? Does it not lurk faintly below the surface, where its vague, scaly skin subtly blends with and intensifies the rippling eddy?

An earlier version of the same passage ends with "a ruffled tree, or the chimney smoke of a house where spinach was cooking" (*Nabokov's Dozen*, p. 132). Though more Goglian—more uneasily humorous—the spinach smoke seems weaker in cumulative green. But it similarly haunts.

An interesting specimen occurs in *Pnin*. After their daughter married "a Waindell graduate with an engineering job in a remote Western state," the Clementses "felt dejected, apprehensive, and lonely in their nice old drafty house that now seemed to hang about them like the flabby skin and flapping clothes of some fool who had gone and lost a third of his weight."[22] Not until the final word "weight" does the simile completely crystallize. In context (the daughter "left" on the preceding page), it is slightly less obvious that "lost weight" refers not only to the empty house, but even more precisely to the lost daughter in a sort of eerie "reverse birth" effect, complete with hanging, flabby skin. Even the not necessarily justified value judgment ("fool") seems to return to flavor the parents' loneliness and dejection.

Of the two "Soviet experts" engaged to locate the Zemblan crown jewels in *Pale Fire*, Kinbote says: "One has seldom seen, at least among waxworks, a pair of more pleasant, presentable chaps. Everybody admired their clean-shaven jaws, elementary facial expressions, wavy hair, and perfect teeth" (p. 173). The haunting return is rapid, easily missed. By the time most readers realize that "at least" has been substituted for "except," they have probably also encountered considerable evidence that these men *are* human waxworks. The phrase "everybody admired" is especially insidious, implying total conformity to awesome standards of gleaming *poshlust*.

These two men are next described by a false contrast similar to that which introduces Gogol's arguing Ivans, whereupon they even seem "early evening" Gogolian Amateurs of Boots: "both wore elegant jackboots of soft black leather, and the sky turned away showing its ethereal vertebrae."

(They are "silhouetted against the now flushed sky.") If the parallels with Gogol are intended, they are now complete with Gogolian reaction to Gogolian *poshlust*. Moreover, the reaction itself derives from a typically eerie reversal of point of view. Similarly, it seems possible that Nabokov spread Gogol's garrison-soldier-uniform sky (which he has translated and discussed[23]) over three places in his own works.[24]

Such tempting potential parallels are numerous. In a corner-room shop of the hotel where Chichikov first stops, there is a man in the window "with a samovar of red copper and a face exactly as red as the samovar, so that from afar one could have thought that in the window were standing two samovars, if one samovar had not been with a black as pitch beard" (6:8). In this translation, I have ruthlessly maintained the Russian word order because it contributes to the humorous reversal. (The words "two samovars" for example, should immediately precede and thereby enhance the deception of "one samovar," which, in turn, should be deprived of the word "beard" as long as possible to sustain the deception.) Nabokov may be seen to stop "prudently" short of a similar reversal in telling us that Mr. Piffke (*King, Queen, Knave*) had "a profile that had prudently stopped halfway between man and teapot" (p. 77). In *The Gift*, one finds "Mme Chernyshevski, becoming for a moment—as usually happens—remarkably similar to her own (blue, gleaming) teapot" (p. 43). Nabokov's world, as he claims, is surely quite different from Gogol's, yet there are similarities—from apparent territorial "reality" to minute verbal ritual.

Nabokov's well-known manipulation of the Hegelian syllogism (see *Laughter in the Dark*, pp. 78–9) is closely allied to his use of the haunting return device. In the syllogism, however, both reversals, or twists of logic, revolve primarily around the initial image. But the final effect is similar: a sudden return opens up fresh, expanded perception.

Parallels in Gogol include both humorous and eerie effects. Of Sobakevich we are told: "No soul whatever seemed to be present in that body, or if he did have a soul it was not where it ought to be, but, as in the case of Kashchey the Deathless [a ghoulish character in Russian folklore] it dwelled somewhere beyond the mountains and was hidden under such a thick crust, that anything that might have stirred in its depths could produce no tremor whatever on the surface." (6:101) The translation and brackets are Nabokov's.[25] The word "or" humorously promotes a false alternative that ultimately corroborates "seemed." The syllogism (no soul, soul, no effective soul) is brief but complete. Its final image vividly rein-

forces the initial assertion, which was tempting, but difficult, to believe.
And our last, and lasting, impression is surely the more convincing for its
almost eerie complexity.

In Part Two of *Dead Souls*, Chichikov learns that Petukh has mort-
gaged his estate because everyone is doing so, and Petukh has no desire
to "lag behind" the others.

> "What a fool, what a fool!" thought Chichikov, "squandering everything and turn-
> ing his children into little splurgers." . . .
> "Oh, I know what you're thinking," said Petukh.
> "What?" asked Chichikov, embarrassed.
> "You're thinking: 'What a fool, what a fool this Petukh is! Invited me to dinner,
> and not a sign of it yet.' " (7:50)

At once both near and far. On the next page, Chichikov demolishes his
food-loving host by admitting that he has already dined. He then consoles
Petukh, however, by saying he had no appetite before and consequently ate
nothing.

Nabokov employs the syllogism more extensively than Gogol, but
similar eerie humor not infrequently redounds:

> STUMP: Ow, ow, ow, my foot is asleep.
> LUMP: Now wait a minute—that's an artificial leg you have here.
> STUMP: Ah, that's what the matter is.[26]

Despite its facetiousness, this syllogistic tweak from Nabokov's play *The
Waltz Invention* does suggest the tingling supposed to exist in appropriate
space, after amputation, with surprising vividness. The subtle pun "matter"
is almost sinisterly Gogolian.

Like Gogol, Nabokov also employs the device with deceptive, deep
seriousness. A short story called "That in Aleppo Once . . ." contains this
passage: "quite suddenly she started to sob in a sympathetic railway carriage. 'The Dog,' she said, 'the dog we left. I cannot forget the poor dog.'
The honesty of her grief shocked me, as we had never had any dog. 'I
know,' she said. 'But I tried to imagine we had actually bought that setter.
And just think, he would be now whining behind a locked door.' There had
never been any talk of buying a setter" (*Nabokov's Dozen*, p. 105). The
irony of "honesty" is intensified by its considerably preceding the dog they
never had. Since the syllogism is here complete (dog, no dog, imagined

dog) even without the concluding sentence, the phrase "never been any talk" seems to remove the imaginary dog yet another distance from "reality." (Even the animal's hypothetical existence was apparently purely imaginary.) And yet, despite the at least double denial of its reality[27] (and partly through selection of vivid detail), the dog perversely seems to whine all the louder.

In both Nabokov and Gogol the syllogism takes the reader back to where he started, only to emphasize that he is now somewhere else. Thus, one is artfully jarred into recognizing one's own perceptual limitations. And whatever humor ensues is characteristically tinged with eerieness.

Both Nabokov and Gogol often depict sudden, perspective-wrenching reflections (in puddles, mirrors, lakes, and so on) which all seem part of a larger and stranger preoccupation with reversing the real and the unreal. Of Akaki Akakievich, Nabokov revealingly finds that "his ghost seems to be the most tangible, the most real part of his being" (*Nikolai Gogol,* p. 146). The people of both Nabokov's and Gogol's worlds relentlessly encounter eerie alterations of "reality"—reversal-like transformations of what had been previously taken for granted. In Gogol's *Portrait,* a strange, vision-like dream seems to contain, deep inside, "a terrifying fragment of reality" (3:92).

When Van Veen does, and yet does not, commit suicide, we read that "his destiny simply forked at that instant, as it probably does sometimes at night, especially in a strange bed, at stages of great happiness or great desolation, when we happen to die in our sleep, but continue our normal existence, with no perceptible break in the faked serialization, on the following, neatly prepared morning, with a spurious past discreetly but firmly attached behind."[28] Beneath its muted facetiousness, this passage subtly but viciously feeds upon its own growing Doubt.[29] Its not unsinister conclusion ("neatly prepared," "discreetly but firmly") is preceded by a disarmingly casual tone ("destiny simply forked," "happen to die in our sleep"). And a long *a* assonance subtly highlights—even though it is termed not "perceptible"—the "break" in "faked serialization."

Further reversals common to both Nabokov and Gogol include basic plot pattern[30] and even an expressed desire to alter authorial voice.[31] But (darkly humorous) disturbing reversals of the real and the unreal seem most characteristic of, and essential to, both writers' worlds. Consider the following two passages (the first ends "Nevsky Prospect," the second is deep in *Speak, Memory*):

. . . everything breathes deception. It is false at any time, this Nevsky Prospect, but
most of all when night descends upon it in a thickening mass, separating the white
and straw-colored walls of the houses, when the entire town turns into thunder and
gleaming light, when streams of carriages cascade from the bridges, . . . and Satan
lights the lamps himself, just to show everything in an unreal aspect. (3:46)

In the purity and vacuity of the less familiar hour, the shadows were on the wrong
side of the street, investing it with a sense of not inelegant inversion, as when one
sees reflected in the mirror of a barbershop . . . a stretch of sidewalk shunting a
procession of unconcerned pedestrians in the wrong direction, into an abstract world
that all at once stops being droll and loosens a torrent of terror. (p. 296))

Both passages effect characteristic perception-expanding reversals.
Whereas Gogol typically has Satan almost playfully make (totally serious)
eerie optical mischief, Nabokov breathes frightening life into his "unconcerned pedestrians" and more deliberately releases his "torrent of terror."
Any resulting humor is typically darker and less playful. Indeed, Nabokov
creates his reversal with a directness evincing the respect he has expressed
for Gogol's art: "At this superhigh level of art, literature . . . appeals to
that secret depth of the human soul where the shadows of other worlds pass
like the shadows of nameless and soundless ships. As one or two patient
readers may have gathered by now, this is really the only appeal that
interests me."[32]

Notes

1. Vladimir Nabokov, *Nikolai Gogol* (New York, 1944), p. 155.

2. *Ibid.*, p. 144.

3. Vladimir Nabokov, "The Art of Fiction," *Paris Review*, No. 41 (1967), p. 106.

4. This evocative transliteration of the Russian word *poshlost'* is Nabokov's. See *Nikolai Gogol*, p. 63, and "The Art of Fiction," p. 103. A long passage in *The Gift* strikingly parallels Nabokov's famous explanation of *poshlust*. For example, "the father with a prize growth on his pleased face, the mother with her imposing bosom; the dog is also looking at the table, and envious Grandma can be seen ensconced in the background" (*The Gift*, New York, 1963, p. 22); "mother clasps her hands in dazed delight, the children crowd around, all agog, Junior and the dog strain up to the edge of the table where the Idol is enthroned; even Grandma of the beaming wrinkles peeps out somewhere in the background" (*Nikolai Gogol*, p. 66).

5. In cases where Nabokov alludes to Gogol, the potential influence seems relatively obvious: "Luzhin was sitting sideways at the table on which, frozen in various poses like the

characters in the concluding scene of Gogol's *The Inspector General*, were the remains of the refreshments, empty and unfinished glasses" (*The Defense*, New York, 1964, p. 232).

6. Not without good reason, perhaps, has Nabokov spoken of Gogol's "Pandora's box mind" (*Nikolai Gogol*, p. 118).

7. *Ibid.*, p. 142. Dmitry Chizhevsky has of course written extensively on Gogol's often astonishing use of the word "even" (*dazhe*). See his "O 'Shineli' Gogolya," *Sovremennye zapiski* (Paris), 67 (1938), pp. 173–4, 178–84. Nabokov also uses the words "even" and "almost" (among others) in a similar way, and he has even revealed the device in his own writing: "Almost nightly—and what monstrous melancholy lurked in that 'almost'—. . . ." (*King, Queen, Knave*, New York, 1968, p. 81.) On the next page: "he perceived almost without looking the tense sheen of her stocking." Consider also the perversely evocative potential of Gradus's stop in a "nice, modern, almost odorless lavatory" (*Pale Fire*, New York, 1966, p. 193), which combines Gogolian *poshlust* ("nice") with faintly disturbing suggestiveness ("almost"). The *poshlusty* "nice" echoes and re-echoes in Gradus's "nice" stay at the Beverland Hotel (p. 195) and his drinking "two paper-cupfuls of nice cold milk from [of course] a dispenser" (p. 198). The word "really" works similarly tainted wonders in *King, Queen, Knave*.

8. *Nabokov's Dozen* (New York, 1958), p. 145, my italics. Also my italics in all the examples that follow, except where noted otherwise.

9. *King, Queen, Knave*, pp. 7, 81, 83.

10. *Laughter in the Dark* (New York, 1966), p. 16.

11. *Despair* (New York, 1966), pp. 20, 71.

12. *Lolita* (New York, 1955), p. 284, and *King, Queen, Knave*, pp. 22, 206. For two more, see *Lolita*, p. 90, and *Tyrants Destroyed and Other Stories* (New York, 1975), p. 66.

13. Gogol, 1:139. For two more, see 3:34, 35.

14. *Pale Fire*, p. 16. For two more, see *Laughter in the Dark*, p. 21, and *The Real Life of Sebastian Knight* (Norfolk, Conn., 1959), p. 28.

15. The translation and italics are Nabokov's (*Nikolai Gogol*, p. 148).

16. Vladimir Nabokov, *The Enchanter*, Trans. Dmitri Nabokov (New York, 1986), p. 59.

17. Jorge Luis Borges, *Labyrinths* (New York, 1964), p. 208.

18. *Despair*, p. 59, and *King, Queen, Knave*, pp. 102, 202.

19. With remarkable accuracy, Nabokov reversely translated "blessed" into Russian as "cursed" (*proklyatoe*) in the Russian version of *Lolita* (New York, 1967), p. 122.

20. With what one suspects may be the natural, if unwitting, symmetry of true genius, inquisitive cockroaches earlier seem to transfer to a nosy hotel neighbor some of their own silent attentiveness (6:8; echoed, 6:174).

21. *Speak, Memory* (New York, 1966), p. 101.

22. *Pnin* (New York, 1965), p. 30.

23. Gogol, 6:23; see Nabokov, *Nikolai Gogol*, p. 78.

24. See V. Nabokov, "The Poets," *TriQuarterly*, Winter 1970, pp. 4–5, and *The Eye* (New York, 1966), pp. 6, 84.

25. *Nikolai Gogol*, p. 98.

26. *The Waltz Invention* (New York, 1966), pp. 53–4.

27. The denial may even be deemed a triple one, since the "narrator" (the story is in

the form of a letter) repeatedly claims that his wife "never existed" (*Nabokov's Dozen*, pp. 103, 109, 111).

28. *Ada* (New York, 1969), p. 445.

29. And thus the treatment may be seen to reach disturbingly on beyond Borges, who raises similar questions, but with much less near-sadistic relish. See, for example, *Labyrinths*, pp. 28, 50.

30. "Gogol's guns," Nabokov writes, "hang in midair and do not go off—in fact the charm of his allusions is exactly that nothing ever comes of them" (*Nikolai Gogol*, p. 44). Humbert's gun does not shoot Lolita, nor Albinus's gun Margot, nor Van's gun himself. Neither is Hermann's "double" his double, the "doomed" Dreyer is not drowned, and so on. Gogol's *Inspector General* ends in an almost inevitable reversal, just as *Dead Souls*—as it has survived and is discussed by its author—evokes a ghostly, projected about-face. Even the famous ending of a Gogol short story—"It is dreary in this world, ladies and gentlemen!" (2:276)—may be taken as a disturbing reversal simply by emphasizing the word "this."

31. "No! . . . I cannot! . . . Give me another pen!" (Gogol, 2:271); ". . . all New England for a lady-writer's pen!" exclaims Humbert (*Lolita*, p. 51).

32. *Nikolai Gogol*, p. 149.

15

On Black Humor in Gogol and Nabokov

Discussions of black humor or black comedy often feature the works
of Vladimir Nabokov but rarely those of Nikolai Gogol. For example, Max
Schulz in "Toward a Definition of Black Humor"[1] refers to Nabokov repeatedly. No doubt one reason for neglect of Gogol is his relative unfamiliarity
for English readers. Yet numerous effects of dark humor produced by these
two very different writers are strikingly similar, Nabokov's disclaimers[2]
notwithstanding.

To begin with, the reversal words favored by both Nabokov and Gogol
(see the preceding chapter) are often darkly humorous. In Gogol's *The
Inspector General*, Dobchinsky makes a request to Khlestakov "regarding a
certain very delicate circumstance" (4:66). His eldest son, he explains,
was conceived before the marriage. But this was done just as "perfectly,"
he hastens to add, as if the marriage had already taken place. Now, having
legalized the situation, he desires permission to call his "lawful" son
"Dobchinsky." The dark humor of "perfectly" (does marriage render con-
ception any more perfect?) is enhanced by what we have learned earlier:
Dobchinsky's belatedly legalized son may well be the judge's (64). The
"very delicate circumstance" is therefore doubly indelicate. In Nabokov's
Lolita, Humbert refers to the girl as his "aging mistress."[3] Lolita is indeed
aging (especially in view of Humbert's predilection for nymphets), but this
description ironically reminds us how disturbingly young this mistress really is.

Doctors, sickness, and hospitals readily lend themselves to effects of
dark humor—for instance, the hospital scenes in Joseph Heller's *Catch
22* and the gynecologist lampoon in Southern and Hoffenberg's *Candy*. In
The Inspector General, the patients at the hospital are said to be "getting

well like flies" (45). The implications are both humorous and disturbing. Not only do the flies reversely suggest "dying like," they also suggest unsanitary hospital conditions. Less playful is Nabokov's frequent depiction of outrageous attitudes of human beings toward one another. Scheming to have Lolita, Humbert imagines for Charlotte (in order to get her out of the way) "a nice Caesarean operation and other complications in a safe maternity ward" (p. 82). The words "nice" and "safe" reverse their meanings when considered from Charlotte's point of view.[4] In *The Enchanter*, the protagonist pictures his bride's "as yet undisclosed miracles of surgery" (she recently had an operation on her intestine): "here his imagination was left hanging on barbed wire."[5] Not only does the selected image ingeniously suggest her scar; it also accords with the man's prison-like confinement with his moribund wife, whom he has married to gain access to her daughter, but who is now "ominously obedient" to his displays of affection. With Gogol, the effect occurs more playfully and less often. Shponka is told by his aunt that he, as a baby, almost soiled her dress, but "fortunately" she handed him to the nurse just in time (1:295). Here "fortunately" reverses itself if we picture the plight of the nurse. When Kovalyov (in "The Nose") returns home after failing to place an ad in the newspaper, he finds his lackey Ivan lying on his back and spitting "rather successfully" at a spot on the ceiling (3:64). Clearly, the word "successfully" reverses itself in context as gravity takes effect.

The last two examples focus on human excreta. Both Nabokov and Gogol repeatedly refer to corporeal functions. In result, the appetites, creations, and eliminations of the human body often seem uneasily animalistic. Coprological detail is typical. In Nabokov's *Despair*, Hermann discovers in the place where the tramp Felix had been "that pathetically impersonal trace which the unsophisticated wanderer is wont to leave under a bush: one large, straight, manly piece and a thinner one coiled over it" (p. 27). The word "manly" is oddly associated with thickness in this description, and it appears just when man is, like an animal, detectable only by his trace. In *Pale Fire*, Kinbote frequently employs "manly" to suggest homosexual activities. Evoking an interest between men, "manly" ironically reverses its customary meaning.

John Barth's Todd Andrews bursts out laughing when he sees himself making love in a large bedroom mirror. "Nothing," he writes, "to me, is so consistently, profoundly, earth-shakingly funny as we animals in the act of mating."[6] In Nabokov's *King, Queen, Knave*, Franz lifts up a strand of

Martha's hair "with a nose-wrinkling horse-nuzzle."[7] The relationship between these two is purely physical, and the image of a nuzzling horse seems quite apt for amorous Franz. In Gogol's "the Carriage" Chertokutsky (awakened by his wife) lets out "a low mooing sound, like a calf emits when seeking with its muzzle the teats of its mother." He then mutters: "Mm . . . Stretch out your little neck, sugar plum. I'll kiss you." (3:187) The amorous husband likened to a calf seeking its mother is not merely animalistic; the description also reminds us that a woman's body accommodates both her lover and her offspring. In *Dead Souls*, Chichikov's carriage collides with another: inside, we see a golden-haired girl whose face is compared to a freshly laid egg (6:90). The idea of giving birth seems rather uneasily introduced here, although there is a certain logic, however unusual in context, in associating male-female relationships with giving birth and nursing. Finally alone with Lolita in a hotel room, Humbert, sexually aroused, retires to the bathroom: "where it took me quite a time to shift back into normal gear for a humdrum purpose" (p. 123). Here, Nabokov suggests with faintly uneasy humor the dual function of the male organ. The word "humdrum," moreover, contains two Nabokovian shimmers of meaning[8]: "Hum" (as he proceeds to inform us) is "drumming" upon the toilet's watery surface. In Gogol's *Inspector General* Dobchinsky—evidently, cuckolded by the judge—has a little girl who is described, in literal translation, as "a poured-out judge" (4:64).

In Gogol's "The Diary of a Madman," Poprishchin's developing madness evinces a near logic which is strangely anticipatory. Dreaming of becoming an important person, he writes: "Just wait . . . I'll yet be a colonel myself, and God willing perhaps something even higher" (3:198). Later, when he believes himself to be the King of Spain, these words acquire a rather biting irony, especially the phrase "God willing." Poprishchin ingeniously construes his painful treatments at the insane asylum as quaint ceremonies honoring the new Spanish King. Nabokov has also treated insanity, with dark humor, as almost frighteningly logical. A favored manifestation of this is termed "referential mania," and it occurs most vividly in *The Defense* and in the short story "Signs and Symbols."

Both Nabokov and Gogol persistently feature taboo topics. *Ada* chronicles incest; *Lolita*, pedophilia. Humbert craftily describes an imaginary adultery to convince the nosy Farlows that Lolita is really his own daughter. She is allegedly the fruit of "a mad love affair" (p. 102) between him and Charlotte, so that after Charlotte's death it is perfectly proper for Lolita to live with Humbert. As he leaves to pick up Lolita at camp, Jean Farlow says, "Kiss your daughter for me" (p. 106). In Gogol's "The Sorochinsk Fair," when Paraska and her father dance together, thinking they are alone, Tsybulya interrupts them: "Well, that's fine, the father and daughter have fixed up a wedding here all by themselves!" (1:135). Earlier in the same story, we see Havronia leading the priest's son to the hut where she is staying. At this point, she is termed Solopi's "mistress." The term is accurate, but it also suggests Havronia's intended relationship with another man. The taboo focus is intensified by the fact that her would-be lover is the priest's son. At the hut he mentions "offerings," adding that only from Havronia can one receive truly delectable offerings. "Here are some offerings for you," answers Havronia, "placing wooden bowls on the table and coyly buttoning up her apparently unintentionally unbuttoned blouse." She goes on to enumerate the doughy foods in the bowls (1:122). The words "apparently unintentionally," of course, suggest an intentional display. "Offerings" with reference to food for a priest's son is ironic. Moreover, before the doughy "offerings" are named, the focus playfully shifts to Harvonia's revealing blouse. The priest's son then says that his heart craves for sweeter foods from Havronia. When she feigns not to understand what food he has in mind, he replies: "Of your love."

The appetite for food is also associated with sexual appetite in *Lolita*. Near the town of Kasbeam, Humbert remarks that Lolita "craved for fresh fruits" (p. 214). He then goes into town to buy her some bananas while she stays at the motel and makes love with Quilty. In view of Lolita's relationship with Humbert, the phrase "craved for fresh fruits" expands in meaning as we realize that she had planned to meet Quilty near Kasbeam. Indeed, Humbert seems to suspect what has happened as he watches her eat one of the bananas.

With both Nabokov and Gogol, the natural functions of the human body are seen in disharmony with social convention. Humbert describes Charlotte as follows: "Oh, she was very genteel: she said 'excuse me' whenever a slight burp interrupted her flowing speech" (p. 77). In *Dead Souls* we learn how "extremely precise and genteel in their words and expressions" the ladies of N are: "They never said, 'I blew my nose,' 'I sweated,' or 'I spat,' but rather conveyed this by 'I relieved my nose' or 'I had to make use of my handkerchief'" (6:158–9).[9] Both writers add playful twists to this pattern. Chichikov impresses a servant at the inn: "In the gestures of this gentleman there was something quite solid, and he blew his nose exceedingly loudly" (6:10). The nose-blowing is comically glorified as gentlemanly and the word "solid" is used to suggest a quite unsolid procedure. Of Nabokov's Pnin, we read: "The zipper a gentleman depends on most would come loose in his puzzled hand at some nightmare moment of haste and despair."[10] Here, "gentleman" seems in humorous disharmony with the physical need referred to—regardless of how the hypothetical gentleman depends on his zipper.

Summarizing the aesthetic strategies of black humor, Schulz notes a careful blurring of the distinction between narrator and author. This allows, he writes, "for the introduction of authorial responses to the narrator's vision not verified by the experience of the narrative" (p. 130). As an example Schulz offers the ending of *Lolita*. From Gogol's works, we may adduce the endings of *Dead Souls* (part 1), the "Ivans" tale, and *The Inspector General*, wherein the narrative (or stage directive) consciousness abruptly soars above what precedes it, leaving the reader (or spectator) with the strange feeling that the point of view to which he has previously been exposed is only one of several possible perspectives. The effect is ironically vivifying, bringing to mind Barbara Monter's phrase "an illusion of *unreality*."[11]

Both Gogol and Nabokov favor a descriptive technique whereby someone or something is inaccurately labeled, promoting the reader's creative participation. Early in *Dead Souls*, we see a window apparently containing two samovars, except that "one samovar" has a pitch-black beard; quick deduction tells us that the word "samovar" refers to a face which, however, resembles a samovar. We also learn that Manilov's son Femistoklius wants to be an ambassador when he grows up. Then a servant wipes "the ambassador's" nose to prevent a large drop from falling into his soup (6:31). In "May Night, or The Drowned Maiden," we read that the village head "was a widower, but in his house lived his sister-in-law" (1:161). The woman is repeatedly called "sister-in-law," while the reader becomes increasingly certain that her role is other than that of a sister-in-law. In "Shponka," the aunt informs her nephew that a certain Stepan Kuzmich allegedly deeded him some land. This man, she tells Shponka, "began to visit your mother when you were not yet in the world; true, at times when your father was not at home" (1:295). Typically, Gogol has the aunt say "your father" just as we learn that Shponka's father was perhaps someone else.

Nabokov also uses inaccurate labeling to suggest furtive sex. During the bedroom scene at the Enchanted Hunters, Lolita talks in her sleep and calls Humbert (who is stealthily approaching the bed) "Barbara." We then read: "Barbara, wearing my pajamas which were much too tight for her, remained poised motionless over the little sleep-talker" (p. 130). Both "Barbara" and "her" are vividly inaccurate. Moreover, Nabokov's wording graphically suggests the physical contrast between males and females. Gogol, in Shponka's dream, brings out this contrast still more sharply by having him discover that "his wife was not a person at all but some kind of woolen material" (1:307). Such a wife, we learn, is usually measured and cut by a merchant. Shponka has already exclaimed that he would not know what to do with a wife (306). His nightmare realization that a female which is a flat woolen area that is measured and cut is "not a person at all" is thus darkly humorous.

In part 2 of *Dead Souls*, Chichikov reflects that it may be possible to avoid repaying the money he has borrowed: "A strange thought presented itself; it was not as if Chichikov had conceived it himself, but it suddenly, all on its own, appeared, teasing, smirking, and winking at him" (7:89). As Humbert plans to drug Lolita in order to fondle her at night, we read: "Other visions of venery presented themselves to me swaying and smiling" (p. 73). In both descriptions, the unsavory ideas seem to come from outside, seductively approaching Chichikov and Humbert, whose guilt seems faintly, humorously diminished.

When Chichikov buys Khlobuev's estate, he pays 10,000 rubles in cash, and another 5,000 are "promised" for delivery the next day: ". . . that is, promised; it was planned to bring three, the rest later, maybe in two or three days, and if possible to postpone it yet somewhat more" (7:86–7). At this point, the word "promised" has been humorously reversed; the money seems almost to appear and then vanish. In *Laughter in the Dark*, the following is offered through the eyes of Axel Rex: "They could have given him a better room for his money (which, he thought, they might never see)."[12] As with Chichikov, the payment seems to appear only to be canceled by subsequent wording.

Both writers employ the device of inaccurate labeling to create a tinge of dark humor when death is concerned. As Akaki's mother ("The Overcoat") tries to decide upon a name for him, she is repeatedly termed "the deceased" (3:142). In *King, Queen, Knave*, Martha and Franz plot to kill Dreyer. As their schemes unfold, he is called "my late husband," "my deceased," and "the deceased" while still alive (pp. 156, 158). "The deceased used to sleep on that bed there," Martha tells Franz. And since two of their schemes entail shooting Dreyer, we are told that (according to the second plan) Franz would be waiting behind a tree with the "reloaded" revolver (p. 179). Nabokov develops the idea still further: "When they had again killed" Dreyer, Franz would "again" take his wallet (1979–80). In *Pale Fire*, Kinbote casually mentions a "self-made widow."[13]

Today it may be difficult to see *Dead Souls* as assaulting a religious taboo, yet the title was originally banned by the censor because of the church's position that souls are eternal and thus cannot be termed dead.[14] But Gogol went still further. Korobochka, we recall, has the eerie presence of mind to wonder if dead souls might somehow be useful around the house. She also inquires if Chichikov wishes to dig the dead souls up out of the ground (6:51). Later there is speculation about the difficulty of resettling Chichikov's souls, including fear of an "uprising" by such a "restless lot" (6:155). In part 2, Tentetnikov speculates that Chichikov is a professor traveling about in search of plants, or perhaps fossilized objects (7:27). Chichikov is of course still seeking to acquire dead souls. The word *iskopaemye* (here rendered "fossilized objects") suggests through its root meaning "dug up things." Also in part 2, Platonov is plagued by intense boredom. Chichikov sympathetically, and hopefully, proposes that this boredom may have been caused by the deaths of many serfs (7:52).

Nabokov derives much of his dark humor about death from suicide. In *Pale Fire* Kinbote writes: "There are purists who maintain that a gentleman should use a brace of pistols, one for each temple" (p. 157). He proceeds to term vein-tapping in one's bath a "fancy release" but "uncertain and messy." "Air comfort" (in jumping from high buildings) is also discussed. "The ideal drop," he concludes, "is from an aircraft, your muscles relaxed . . . your packed parachute shuffled off, cast off, shrugged off—farewell, *shootka!*" This Zemblan word is translated by Kinbote as "little chute." Also aptly, it is spelled like the English word *shoot*. Still another play of meaning derives from the Russian *shutka* ("joke"): the implication is that life itself may be a joke which is shrugged off by the gesture of suicide. Indeed, Kinbote's mockingly glorified tone ("purists," "ideal drop") seems mixed with disturbing suggestions of pleasure, of escape ("fancy release," "air comfort," "muscles relaxed"). If life is seen as a brief, deceptive condition limited by the range of normal conscious perception, the idea of release or escape can turn grimly serious. In *Speak, Memory* Nabokov writes: "The prison of time is spherical and without exits. Short of suicide, I have tried everything."[15] And if death is apparently viewed by Nabokov as an escape, or release, we may recall that in Gogol's

"The Overcoat" Akaki finally "releases" his ghostly soul (*ispustil dukh*, 3:168).

In sum, both Gogol and Nabokov persistently, and often rather playfully, touch upon subjects generally considered improper, indelicate, even taboo. This has produced some strikingly similar effects of dark humor. Such humor, by twisting or reversing generally accepted attitudes and values, tends to undermine the reader's world. Sex, insanity, and death are uneasily featured. With both writers, the natural functions of the human body are seen in disharmony with social convention. Ultimately human life and even its termination are viewed from a faintly alien perspective. The process is reinforced by ironic reversals of individual words. Additional perspectives are abruptly added by what Schulz terms "authorial responses to the narrator's vision not verified by the experience of the narrative." And the technique of inaccurate labeling promotes the reader's vivifying participation. Despite these various similarities, we may note some differences in emphasis. Nabokov more frequently depicts an outrageous attitude of one human being towards another. With Nabokov the human body seems more animalistic; medical care is more grimly undermined. With Gogol insanity seems a relatively playful (though nonetheless painful) internal disorder; Nabokov presents it as a sinister conspiracy from without. Gogolian humor relating to death seems relatively muted and capricious; Nabokov insinuates a disturbing attraction towards suicide. We may also discern a difference in overall effect. Dark humor seems more consciously contrived by Nabokov. It seems more basic to the world view promoted by his writing—a view however from which he seeks to dissociate himself. With Gogol even the most similar effects seem less pessimistic, though they may condition a more resigned perspective on human life. In short, one can discern Gogol's sad smile as he walks hand in hand with his characters,[16] whereas Nabokov's characters, as he has claimed, are indeed galley slaves.[17]

Notes

1. *Southern Review*, 9 (1973), pp. 117–34. Schulz refers to Nabokov four times in proposing "six kinds of deployment" relating to "the aesthetic strategies of Black Humor" (p. 130). See also Mathew Winston, "*Humour noir* and Black Humor," in: Harry Levin, ed., *Veins of Humor* (Cambridge, Mass., 1972), pp. 269–84. Winston focuses on Nabokov in describing "grotesque," as opposed to "absurd" black humor, and the grotesque, via

Victor Erlich's *Gogol* (New Haven, 1969), surely reminds us of Gogol. Winston notes that his label "grotesque" roughly corresponds to Robert Scholes's "picaresque," as distinguished from "satirical" black humor (p. 277). Schulz has found that Scholes minimizes the Black humorists' "seriousness" when he characterizes them as "playful or artful" in some respects (p. 133).

2. See Chapter 14, above.

3. Vladimir Nabokov, *Lolita* (New York, 1955), p. 192.

4. Similarly, Hermann tells us that he was "winding up the brief series of preparatory caresses" in lovemaking that his wife "was supposed to be entitled to." (Vladimir Nabokov, *Despair*, New York, 1966, p. 37.)

5. Vladimir Nabokov, *The Enchanter*, Trans. Dmitri Nabokov (New York, 1986), p. 55.

6. John Barth, *The Floating Opera* (New York, 1967), p. 124.

7. Vladimir Nabokov, *King, Queen, Knave* (New York, 1968), p. 155.

8. See my *Nabokov & Others: Patterns in Russian Literature* (Ann Arbor, 1979), pp. 155–64.

9. This sort of dark humor reaches its peak—or nadir—in J. P. Donleavy's *The Gingerman* (New York, 1959) when Sebastian Dangerfield defends his friend Kenneth to his wife Marian: "Kenneth's a gentleman in every respect. Have you ever heard him fart?" (p. 42.) Douglas Davis has called Sebastian Dangerfield "perhaps the best case study" of black humor heroes. (Douglas M. Davis, ed., *The World of Black Humor*, New York, 1967, p. 18.)

10. Vladimir Nabokov, *Pnin* (New York, 1965), p. 14.

11. Barbara Heldt Monter, " 'Spring in Fialta': The Choice that Mimics Chance," *TriQuarterly*, 17 (Winter 1970), p. 133.

12. Vladimir Nabokov, *Laughter in the Dark* (New York, 1966), p. 78.

13. Vladimir Nabokov, *Pale Fire* (New York, 1966), p. 60. Somewhat similarly, Charles Addams has shown a multitude of gravestones for sale and the sign, "Special! Do-it-yourself kit." In J. P. Donleavy's *A Fairy Tale of New York* (New York, 1973), the hero dreams of building "an empire of bargain-priced self-service funeral parlors" (p. 85). And in John Barth's *The Floating Opera* there is a 90-year-old lady "who buys her one-a-day vitamin pills in the smallest bottles—for her, the real economy size" (p. 50).

14. See Gogol's letter to P. A. Pletnev, 7 Jan. 1842 (12:28).

15. Vladimir Nabokov, *Speak, Memory* (New York, 1966), p. 20. The Russian version reads: "Kazhetsya, krome samoubijstva, ya pereproboval vse vykhody." (Vladimir Nabokov, *Drugie berega*, New York, 1954, p. 10.)

16. Gogol suggests this early in chapter 7 of *Dead Souls* (6:134).

17. "The Art of Fiction, XL: Vladimir Nabokov, an Interview," *Paris Review*, 41 (summer-fall 1967), p. 96.

16

The Motif of Falling in *A Hero of Our Time*

The leading adjective applied by Vladimir Nabokov to Lermontov as the author of *A Hero of Our Time* is "energetic," and he further emphasizes "the superb energy of the tale."[1] As Richard Freeborn puts it, "we are plunged into the racing current of Lermontov's prose."[2] John Mersereau states that the hero Pechorin "is energetic, thriving on conflict."[3] John Garrard calls him "one of the most dynamic and enigmatic figures in all of Russian fiction."[4] Boris Eikhenbaum sees Pechorin "in continuous motion, and in each new place a mortal danger awaits him."[5] As I shall attempt to show, the motif of falling artistically intensifies the energy and action that permeate Lermontov's novel.

In each of the three chapters comprising Pechorin's journal, he comes close to death in a climactic encounter. Each time, falling is featured. In "Taman," when the girl attempts to push Pechorin into the water, he crashes down against the side of the boat (4:65). He then causes her to fall into the waves. Prior to the duel with Grushnitski, Pechorin stipulates that they receive fire on the very edge of a precipice: "The one who is wounded will surely fall down headlong and be dashed to pieces." (134) Grazed by a bullet, he does almost drop to his death. As in "Taman," however, it is Pechorin's adversary who finally falls. In "The Fatalist," the hero himself dives headfirst through the window of a hut while trying to capture Efimich alive.

Each of these fall-featuring conflicts is dramatically preceded by a falling object. In the boat Pechorin's pistol, lifted by the girl, falls with a splash into the water. This causes the hero to realize her intention: ". . . a terrible suspicion stole into my soul! The blood rushed to my head . . . I could not swim!" (65) At the duel, a tossed-up silver coin (that gives

Grushnitski the first shot) provides the dramatic focus: "The coin soared up and fell, ringing; everyone rushed toward it." (136) In "The Fatalist," it is precisely when a tossed-up ace of hearts falls to the table that Vulich tests his fate (which inspires Pechorin to make a similar test by trying to take Efimich alive). "Everyone held his breath; all eyes . . . ran back and forth from the pistol to the fateful ace, which, quivering in the air, slowly descended." (150) The word "fateful" (*rokovomu*), which modifies the ace, is also applied to the window through which Pechorin dives (155).

In each case, the person who causes the object to fall is closely involved with what follows. Dr. Werner, who tosses up the coin at the duel, removes the bullet from Grushnitski's body and helps to hush up the incident. In "The Fatalist," Pechorin himself tosses up the ace of hearts in the episode that inspires his own fate-testing dive through the window.[6] In "Taman," it is the girl who drops Pechorin's pistol into the water before she is forced to follow it.

A complex pattern of falling and near falling in the novel involves the association of people with animals. In "Bela," when Kazbich realizes that his precious horse Karagyoz has been stolen, he dashes out "like a wild panther" (23) and runs along the road in pursuit—to no avail. Realizing that he may have lost Vera forever, Pechorin rushes out "like a madman" (141) and gallops off down the road in pursuit—also to no avail. Upon realizing the futility of pursuit, both men fall to the ground and sob. In Pechorin's case, his horse "crashes" to the ground in exhaustion, where-upon: "Exhausted by the day's agitations and by insomnia, I fell on the wet grass and began crying like a child." (142) After losing Karagyoz, Kazbich "fell on the ground and began to sob like a child" (23). When they fall, both Kazbich and Pechorin lie motionless on the ground for a long time. The two episodes are further linked by the fact that it was Pechorin who had arranged for Karagyoz to be stolen. Before this, Kazbich had allowed himself fall into a deep ravine in order to save Karagyoz from falling (18). In the parallel pursuit episode, Pechorin loses his own horse, whereupon he, like the horse, falls from exhaustion. Kazbich, moreover, was unsuc-cessfully interested in Bela, and Karagyoz is said to have "eyes no less beautiful than Bela's" (17). Pechorin was also unsuccessfully attracted to a girl (in "Taman"), whose appearance he associated with a horse: "breed-ing in women, as in horses, is a great thing" (62).

Near the end of "Bela," Kazbich rides another horse,[7] which falls when a bullet breaks its hind leg (40), whereupon he barely escapes alive.

At the duel, Pechorin himself barely avoids death when a bullet grazes him in the leg: ". . . if I had been wounded in the leg a little harder, I would surely have fallen from the cliff." (137) Moreover, it was Pechorin who shot the leg of Kazbich's horse—and Pechorin is himself described like one: ". . . a sign of breeding in a man, like a black mane and a black tail on a white horse." (50)

In "The Fatalist," Vulich is vividly associated with the pig that Efimich also slashes in two, but Lermontov does not explicitly describe the falling of their bodies. However, he further links the two corpses by having Pechorin, who thought he had "read" Vulich's death on his face, muse about his apparent error when he stumbles over the fallen pig (152).

To sum up thus far: several important instances of falling in the novel involve suggestive associations of people with animals. As we have also seen, falling objects precede the falling of three characters in climactic episodes: a pistol (the girl), a coin (Grushnitski), and a playing card (Pechorin).

This last pattern includes several metaphorical fallings. The hero's downfall in "Taman" (robbed by a blind boy, nearly drowned by a young girl) is suggested as follows: "Like a stone thrown into a smooth pool of water, I had disturbed their peace and, like a stone, had nearly gone to the bottom myself!" (66–7) This is preceded by a "falling coin" that rings against a stone—Yanko's unaccepted parting gift to the boy. The ringing "against a stone" provides a smooth connection between the falling coin and the metaphorical stone.[8]

Early in "Princess Mary," Pechorin watches as Grushnitski lets his drinking glass fall to the ground (73). Princess Mary rushes over and recovers it for the posturing invalid—a scene treasured by both participants and mocked by Pechorin in a sequence of events leading to Princess Mary's downfall (and, of course, Grushnitski's as well). Pechorin suggests Princess Mary's downfall by describing a "young soul" as a flower that should be plucked: ". . . and after inhaling one's fill of it, one should throw it away on the road: perhaps someone will pick it up!" (101) This completes the second part of a complex pattern of parallel imagery. The metaphorical fallen flower suggesting Princess Mary's downfall was preceded by the falling glass; a metaphorical falling stone, preceded by the falling coin, had suggested the downfall of Pechorin himself. Moreover, by falling for Grushnitski's ruse and retrieving "the famous glass" (84), Princess Mary had revealed her susceptibility to the sort of romantic role that Pechorin would later play more successfully than Grushnitski.

The other falling coin, the one that precedes Grushnitski's (fatal and literal) downfall, may be associated with still another metaphorical falling object. "So many times," Pechorin declares, "I have played the role of an axe in the hands of fate! Like an executioner's tool, I would fall upon the heads of doomed victims . . ." (129) He writes these lines just a few hours before killing Grushnitski.

Earlier in "Princess Mary," Pechorin theorized about his relationship to other people. "To be always on the alert . . . to destroy plots, to pretend to be fooled, and suddenly, with one shove, to upset the entire huge, carefully wrought structure of cunning and scheming—that is what I call life." (111) "An 'upset structure' aptly describes Pechorin's ultimate effect upon others, and it is the more devastating for his first "pretending to be fooled." He thrives on danger, to the point of creating it for himself. After Vera's note "falls" at his feet (121), Pechorin visits her even though he is twice aware that someone is following him. While leaving, he is ambushed and almost shot: a smoking wad "falls" at his feet (123). Yet he not only escapes but even "knocks down" the Captain of Dragoons.

Maksim Maksimich also suffers a sort of downfall at the hands of Pechorin. He is crushed by the hero's coolly casual attitude when they are reunited. Asked about Pechorin's papers, Maksim Maksimich proceeds to throw, successively, ten notebooks on the ground "with contempt" (53). Not only does the old soldier's action aptly reflect his emotions; these falling papers comprise the greater part of Lermontov's novel, which can thus be considered to fall within itself.

Pechorin is also a major cause of Bela's downfall. Sad that his ardor is cooling, the girl tries desperately to appear cheerful: "but this also did not last; she again fell on the bed and covered her face with her hands" (35). Pechorin explains his lack of constancy as follows: "There is no feminine gaze that I would not forget at the sight of mountains . . . the blue sky, or at the sound of a torrent, falling from crag to crag." (88) "The passions," he later declares, "belong to the young in heart . . . Many peaceful rivers begin as thundering waterfalls, but none tumbles and foams all the way to the sea." (101–2) Still later, he again associates romantic love with falling water (114).

From the very beginning of the novel, instances of falling are anticipated and intensified by references to cliffs, peaks, summits, gorges, chasms, ravines, etc.—and to the possibility that someone may fall. In "Bela," for example, the horses "keep falling" (32) on the mountainous terrain, and Maksim Maksimich remarks that "at any moment, one can expect to fall into a chasm" (33). This is of course precisely what Grushnitski eventually does. "I feel that some day we shall collide on a narrow path, and one of us will fare ill," Pechorin declares (70). This has a double echo: Grushnitski stumbles while ascending a "narrow" trail to the "narrow" dueling platform (134–5). At this point, Pechorin ominously cautions him not to "fall beforehand." He himself then begins to feel dizzy as he looks down, noting that "mossy jags of rocks, cast down by storm and time, awaited their prey." After Grushnitski does in fact fall upon the expectant jags, one may be tempted to make a connection, as the Nabokov commentary does,[9] between Pechorin's noticing Grushnitski's corpse (139) and Pechorin's noticing the body of his horse (145). This is particularly so because the horse had also stumbled (141) prior to its fall and death.

The notion of almost falling also plays a minor role in the drama of Princess Mary's downfall. She becomes deeply indebted to Pechorin when, as he puts it, he "saved her from fainting" (95). Cornered by a drunk who has been incited to embarrass her, Princess Mary is "ready to fall into a faint" (94) when Pechorin rescues her. Still later, crossing a rapid stream on horseback, Princess Mary says "I feel faint!" and Pechorin advises her to look up, away from the water (116–7).

The leitmotif of almost falling recurs at three other times. Vera writes to Pechorin that she "almost fell senseless" (140) upon learning that he was about to duel and that she was the cause of it. Pechorin himself tells us, while proving to Princess Mary that she "cannot love" him, that he came close to falling at her feet (145). Finally, Pechorin declares that he "very nearly fell, having stumbled over something fat and soft" (152); the "something," it develops, was the fallen pig that prefigured Vulich's parallel fate.

As we have seen, the motif of falling (including near falling and potential falling) consistently intensifies the action and the element of danger in *A Hero of Our Time*. Indeed, falling can be seen as a metaphor for the hero's need to intensify his aliveness by deliberately placing himself in out-of-control situations and then tapping his inner reserves of energy. More generally, the motif of falling extends from the characters themselves to several animals and a variety of real and metaphorical objects. It is artistically integral to Lermontov's novel as well. Three of the real falling objects (a pistol, a silver coin, an ace of hearts) are dramatically focused upon prior to climactic episodes that feature falling by the hero and others. The silver coin and two other falling objects (the "famous glass," Yanko's coin) can be associated with three metaphorical ones (the falling axe, the discarded flower, the sinking stone) which, in turn, have a richly suggestive relevance to the downfalls of Grushnitski, Princess Mary, and Pechorin, respectively.

Notes

1. Mikhail Lermontov, *A Hero of Our Time*, Trans. Vladimir Nabokov in collaboration with Dmitri Nabokov (New York, 1958), pp. *xiii, xix*.

2. Richard Freeborn, *The Rise of the Russian Novel* (London, 1973), p. 40.

3. John Mersereau, Jr., *Mikhail Lermontov* (Carbondale, Ill., 1962), p. 150.

4. John Garrard, *Mikhail Lermontov* (Boston, 1982), p. 2 of Preface (not numbered).

5. B. M. Eikhenbaum, *Stat'i o Lermontove* (Leningrad, 1961), pp. 263–4.

6. The role played by fate with Pechorin and Vulich is potentially quite complex. Not only does Vulich seem destined to die even though he, like Pechorin, "tests fate" successfully; we are explicitly told that Efimich might not even have noticed Vulich, had the latter not stopped abruptly and accosted him. Pechorin, on the other hand, is apparently saved from being slashed by the same sabre that killed both Vulich and the pig because of the very smoke created by Efimich's attempt to shoot him. Fate thus seems as determined to ensnare Vulich as to protect Pechorin. Maksim Maksimich, who seems to understand very little about "predestination," ends the novel by unwittingly reinforcing this. The pistol used by Vulich, he suggests, was rather unreliable anyway, but the sabre deserves great respect.

7. It belonged to Bela's father, and Kazbich "threw him to the ground" to obtain it (28).

8. The stone images recurs elsewhere in connection with Pechorin. In "Princess Mary," his heart "turns to stone" (121) at the prospect of marriage; upon seeing Grushnitski's corpse, he says, "a stone was on my heart" (139); and, while parting from Doctor Werner: "I remained as cold as stone" (143).

9. Nabokov translation, p. 210.

17

Deadly Joking in Pushkin and Lermontov

Remarkably often, both Pushkin and Lermontov mention "joking" at serious and important moments in their works. We shall trace the patterning of this phenomenon and attempt to describe its artistic function or effect. All examples will contain the noun *shutka* ("joke") and/or the verb *shutit'* ("to joke").

At the climax of Pushkin's "The Shot," Silvio aims his pistol at the Count, and the latter's bride appears. "Can't you see that we are joking?" the Count tells her (6:100). "Is it true that you are both joking?" she asks Silvio. "He always jokes, Countess," Silvio replies. "Once he jokingly slapped my face, jokingly shot through my cap, jokingly just missed me a moment ago; and now, I'm feeling the urge to joke." Silvio is of course sarcastic, but also deadly serious. Though he chooses to spare the Count, Silvio's accurate shooting of a picture on the wall makes it clear that he could easily have killed him—much as Lermontov's Vulich ("The Fatalist"), after placing a pistol against his head and pulling the trigger (also termed a "joke") eloquently shoots through the center of a cap on the wall.

In "The Queen of Spades," when Hermann presses the Countess to reveal her gambling secret, she replies: "It was a joke. I swear to you, it was a joke!" (6:340) Hermann retorts that "to joke" about such things is impossible; he then causes her death. While all this happens, Lizaveta is sitting in her room recalling how Tomski kept "joking" at the ball about her fondness for engineers (343). "Several of his jokes," we are told, were so accurate that Lizaveta feared he knew "her secret." This secret, of course, has enabled Hermann to reach the Countess. Lizaveta recalls Tomski's "joking" about Hermann as the perpetrator of "at least three acts of villainy" just before Hermann comes to her room and also immediately after he confesses to causing the Countess' death. The almost uncanny accuracy of Tomski's jokes may be seen to complement suggestions that mysterious forces are operating elsewhere in Pushkin's story.

As "The Stationmaster" begins, we encounter a "joking" (6:129) suggestion that people in this profession are dictators. The immediate irony is that stationmasters are roundly abused; the one in Pushkin's tale, moreover, is a sorry dictator indeed: he will be utterly powerless to recover his daughter. (His first name, Samson, intensifies the irony.) When Minski recovers from his feigned illness, we are told that he "joked incessantly, now with Dunya, now with the stationmaster" (136). These jokes, calculated to win the stationmaster's confidence, contribute to the loss of his daughter and, ultimately, of his life.

At the end of "The Snowstorm," Burmin cannot marry Marya Gavrilovna because he once frivolously married someone else. Unaware that his bride was in fact Marya, he confesses—adding that he cannot locate the person "at whose expense I joked so cruelly and who is now so cruelly avenged." (6:118)

Pushkin's use of "deadly joking" in *Dubrovski* amplifies the novel's theme of cruelty and injustice. First, a "joke" (6:221) by Troekurov's huntsman suggests that his master's hounds live better than some neighboring landowners. Andrei Dubrovski writes to Troekurov that he cannot endure such "jokes" (221); this leads, via an ugly legal battle, to the loss of Dubrovski's estate and to his death. A "keen joke" (249) by the police superintendent then implies that Shabashkin will sexually abuse the peasant women on the estate; the peasants respond by burning the two men to death.

Troekurov favors "jokes" involving bears: guests are placed in a cart to which bears have been harnessed and sent on their merry way. "An even better joke" (261) consists of locking a person in a room with a half-starved bear whose chain reaches everywhere except one corner. The scratched and bleeding guest must then remain in that corner for three whole hours. When Troekurov does this to his son's French tutor, he is "astonished by the ending of his joke"—the tutor (Vladimir Dubrovski in disguise) calmly shoots the bear.

Troekurov's "joking" (267) also results in Dubrovski's robbing Spitsyn, who had been a victim of the bear "jokes" as well (272). Finally Vereiski, "joking" about his gout, contrives to ride in a carriage with Marya (291)—an ominous anticipation of his forcing himself upon her in marriage.

Lermontov's *Vadim* is also an unfinished novel wherein the vengeful hero works incognito for the man who has stolen his father's estate and caused his father's death. When Boris Petrovich meets Vadim, he "jokes" (4:168) about Vadim's name, unaware that Vadim intends to kill him. Vadim then tells his sister Olga that he may be "joking" (171) about a secret which, however, he soon reveals as grim fact: Boris Petrovich caused their father's death. Still later, the people near the church believe that Vadim is "joking" (218) when he pushes an old woman, but he has killed her.

Early in *A Hero of Our Time*, Maksim Maksimich learns that Bela is Pechorin's prisoner. "What kind of joking is this?" he asks, demanding Pechorin's sword (4:24). Pechorin then wins Bela's affections by vividly threatening to go off to his death; he does this, Maksim reports, "jokingly" (28). In "The Fatalist," Pechorin also "jokingly" (148) proposes the wager to Vulich about predestination. (The Russian is *shutya* in both cases.) And as Vulich prepares to place the pistol against his head, someone declares: "What an urge to joke!" (149) "A stupid joke!" exclaims another. The symmetry between "The Fatalist" and "Bela"[1] thus includes the following: Pechorin "jokingly" tells Bela that he may go off to his death, but it is she who dies; Pechorin could die in a test of fate inspired by the one he "jokingly" proposes to Vulich, but it is Vulich who dies.

In "Princess Mary," Pechorin overhears the plot to test his courage in a duel with unloaded pistols, including Grushnitski's remark that he "likes to joke his way out." (118) Upon returning home, Pechorin repeatedly declares: "Take care, Mr. Grushnitski! They don't joke with me like that." (120) Then, after deciding that the matter has gone beyond "the limits of a joke" (127), he duels with Grushnitski and kills him.

Long before the duel (apparently fought over Princess Mary), Pechorin mockingly speculates that she already loves Grushnitski. "You always joke!" Grushnitski replies (83), and he later warns Pechorin not to "joke" about his love (96). In conversation with Princess Mary, Pechorin disparages various people: "I began jokingly—and ended with sincere malice." (103) This prompts Princess Mary to declare that Pechorin is "worse" than a murderer.

Some of the above, and other, references to "joking" in Lermontov's novel are perhaps inevitably lost in translation. Even in the Nabokov version, for example, "What an urge to joke!" (of Vulich) becomes "Stop fooling!"—and Pechorin's "They don't joke with me like that" becomes "I am not to be trifled with like this."[2] It should be noted, however, that both these usages are idiomatic.[3]

The references to joking in *Eugene Onegin* are less frequent than in *A Hero of Our Time*, but they function similarly. Indeed, Pushkin also relates joking to the hero's dangerous flirtations and to the climactic duel in which he kills his friend.

First, we read that Eugene's French tutor taught the boy "everything jokingly" (5:10). Remarkably early, the hero learned the art of flirtation— "to astonish innocence jokingly" (13). Later, Onegin's very language is characterized as "half joke, half bile" (29).

The novel's climactic duel has a complex chain of causes: the hero kills Lenski after the latter challenges him because he has flirted with Olga to avenge being deceived about the size of the Larins' party to which he is invited after Lenski takes him to meet Olga because Onegin asks Lenski to do so. When he asks, Lenski replies: "You are joking." (56) Onegin denies it, and the fateful sequence of events has begun.

At the Larins', of course, Onegin also meets Tatiana, who falls in love with him *ne shutya* (66)—"not jokingly," which Nabokov aptly renders "in dead earnest."[4] This and other idiomatic negated expressions are (perhaps necessarily) often altered in translation.[5]

Meanwhile, the Larins' neighbors have been "joking" that Tatiana will marry Onegin (57). But, as Pushkin puts it, "Satan jokes with love" (85): Onegin rejects Tatiana's love, and his idle flirtation at the party leads him to kill his Romantic friend. Zaretski, Lenski's second for the duel, is, appropriately, an expert at inciting young friends to duel—or, having reconciled them, at slandering them both secretly, "with a jolly joke" (122)— presumably, a "joke" suggesting that they cravenly agreed to the reconciliation. Lenski, moreover, fears that Onegin will "joke his way out" (124) of the duel in which he, Lenski, is soon to die. As we have seen, Grushnitski has precisely the same (ironic) fear in *A Hero of Our Time*.

References to joking in Lermontov's poetry often suggest a serious threat to love, peace, and happiness. Both sexes are seen to love "jokingly" (1:209, 303); however, even to utter the name of another's beloved is considered "joking" about something "sacred" (206). Napoleon has "joked with the blood of peaceful citizens, scorned friendship and love, and not trembled before the Creator" (104). One of Lermontov's most famous poems, "It's Both Boring and Sad," ends with the statement that life, if one looks coldly about, "is such an empty and stupid joke" (37). Pushkin's poem "A Scene From *Faust*" also begins with a declaration that the speaker (Faust) is "bored" (*skuchno*). Mephistopheles answers that "the coffin, yawning, awaits us all. So you yawn too." Faust exclaims: "A dry joke!" (2:283) In Lermontov's poem "The Tambov Treasurer's Wife," we are told, of Captain Garin:

> Jokingly once after an argument
> He planted a bullet in the forehead of a friend;
> Jokingly he himself would lie down in a coffin. (2:29)

Other examples may be found in "Song of the Merchant Kalashnikov" (18), "Ismail Bei" (264), and "Hadji Abrek" (352).

Serious joking in Pushkin's poetry focuses upon love, honor, and death. In *Poltava*, when Kochubei is tortured, he bitterly declares that he has lost his honor. Orlik considers this a "joke" (4:281)—and threatens him with more torture. In "Angelo," when Isabela refuses to save her brother's life by submitting to Angelo's desire, he counters by suggesting that she had considered her brother's sin "a joke" (4:363). In "The Water Nymph," a monk watches a naked woman emerge from a lake. She "kisses from afar, jokingly" (1:364), and soon we realize that she has lured the monk to his watery death.

In Pushkin's dramatic works, serious joking focuses upon love and death. In *The Stone Guest*, Don Juan jokingly invites the statue of De Solva (that stands above De Solva's grave) to his tryst with the man's widow. "What an urge to joke," says Leporello, "and with whom!" (5:398) The statue then avenges itself upon Don Juan. In *The Water Nymph*, when the Prince tells the miller's daughter that he cannot see her any more, she accuses him of "joking an empty joke"[6] with her (5:430). She then drowns herself. In *Mozart and Salieri*, the great composer tells his friend that he wishes to treat him to "an unexpected joke" (5:359). He then has a blind musician play some "Mozart" for Salieri; incensed, Salieri poisons him. Other examples can be found in *The Covetous Knight* (5:340) and *Boris Godunov* (5:252).

Lermontov's play *The Masquerade* contains twenty-two references to joking. Several of these involve the honor of various characters—a deadly serious consideration. Three early "jokes" involve the Prince's confusion of the (masked) Baroness with Nina (3:23, 27); his exclamation "It's an evil joke!" is unwittingly prophetic. Three others refer to Arbenin's conversation with a male mask who predicts "misfortune" (24, 25). Arbenin himself "jokes" (29) about the Prince's flirtation—which soon appears to have been with Nina. When Arbenin threatens to kill both himself and Nina, she declares that he is "joking" (40). Still later, the Baroness deplores the Prince's readiness "to joke with a woman's honor" (51).

Finally, when Arbenin poisons Nina and refuses to call a doctor, she says: "You're joking, of course—but it's ungodly to joke that way." (97) As she dies, Arbenin says: "Hell itself cannot joke with my love that way!" (102) Still later, he laments that the Prince "jokingly" took his wife away (105). Finally, accused of murdering his wife, Arbenin replies that he was "jokingly" deceived (112). And upon hearing that Nina was innocent, he says: "You have a great supply of jokes!" (113)

References to joking in Lermontov's other plays function similarly. In *People and Passions*, for example, Yuri indicates a pistol and declares: "My last joke is here." Zarutski says: "Oh! That's a lot for a joke," Interrupting the duel, Lyubov repeatedly says that Yuri must be "joking" (3:280). When his father insults him, Yuri says: "You must be joking . . . such jokes have recently weighed too heavily upon my heart." (288) "I'm joking!" his father sarcastically replies—and then curses Yuri, who kills himself. In *The Strange Man*, when Vladimir hears that Natasha is planning to marry Belinski, he asks her if it is "a joke or not" (3:357). Even though she says it is not, Vladimir continues: "I'm not in a condition now to accept such jokes." He soon loses his mind and dies.

As we have seen, both Pushkin and Lermontov frequently refer to joking at serious and pivotal moments in both their poetry and prose. This tends to promote a sense of cynicism and ironic detachment. Life itself is perceived as vulnerable, precarious, even arbitrary. At the extreme, Fate appears to be mocking the characters, whose honor must nonetheless be defended against potentially fatal jests. "Satan jokes with love," Pushkin wittily suggests. Life is "an empty, stupid joke," Lermontov bitterly declares. Throughout the works of both, "jokes" about life and love have serious or even lethal consequences that are also often termed "joking." Circumstances range from social banter about flirtations and rivalries to duels, torture, and executions. "Honor" is usually a main consideration; boredom often seems a contributing factor. Vulich's joking test of fate, jokingly proposed, and Silvio's joking retaliation for a joking bullet through his hat are characteristic. Pushkin's uses of serious joking are relatively versatile—appropriate for the atmosphere and action within a particular work; Lermontov's seem more uniformly cynical and sarcastic. Finally, one may wonder why, among major Russian writers, Pushkin and Lermontov seem unique in their use of "deadly joking." A major factor: the literary focus was soon to shift to explorations of social issues, with emphasis upon how we should live our lives, and writers were less apt to feature joking at serious moments. Indeed, an emphasis upon how to live one's life seems quite at variance with an honor-dictated obligation to put one's life at risk.

Notes

1. See my *Nabokov & Others: Patterns in Russian Literature* (Ann Arbor, 1979), pp. 33–4.

2. Mikhail Lermontov, *A Hero of Our Time*, Trans. Vladimir Nabokov in collaboration with Dmitri Nabokov (New York, 1958), pp. 186, 147.

3. For Lermontov's 24 uses of "joking," several of which are idiomatic, the Nabokovs have "joke" 7 times and "jest" 6. In one instance, the joking becomes negated: Maksim Maksimich's "What kind of joking is this?" (when he demands Pechorin's sword) becomes "It's no time for joking." (p. 23) The Russian reads: *"Chto za shutki?"* (24)

4. Alexandr Pushkin, *Eugene Onegin*, Trans. with a Commentary, by Vladimir Nabokov (Princeton, N.J., 1975), 1:161.

5. I have generally omitted them. Onegin's dying uncle is said to have fallen "gravely" ill (*ne v shutku*); Pechorin twice angers Princess Mary *ne na shutku* (75, 81), and she asks him "not jokingly" (*ne shutya*) to cut her throat with a knife rather than speak ill of her (103).

6. The expression is idiomatic, but its meaning should be clear. In Pushkin's *The Captain's Daughter*, Pyotr Andreich tells Pugachyov that he is "playing a dangerous game"—literally, "joking a dangerous joke" (6:476). Pugachyov's "joke" has already killed numerous people.

18

Fateful Relationships in "The Queen of Spades"

Pushkin's most complex story haunts the reader with hints of possible interpretations. Its concise, vivid action speeds us through a chronological labyrinth of potentially significant details. Were parts of the story fated to occur? Do supernatural forces, faintly discernible, operate throughout?[1] We may also wonder if everything happens as the characters perceive it. Does the queen of spades, for example, really "screw up her eyes" as it "seems" (6:355) to Hermann at the climax of the story?

From the beginning, Hermann and the Countess are associated by parallel situations and details. They are introduced to the reader together, linked by the fact that both somewhat strangely avoid gambling. Moreover, their abstinence is symmetrical. Hermann longs to gamble but refuses to take the risk; the Countess allegedly possesses a risk-free method, yet enigmatically appears indifferent.[2] Before they meet, Hermann and the Countess are each focused upon separately and somewhat symmetrically. Hermann is so fascinated by the story of her secret that it does not leave his mind the entire night (331); the next night, it dominates his dream of gambling. As we realize only later, the Countess penetrates Lizaveta's thoughts of Hermann: "Who is there to captivate? . . . there was no reason to get all dressed up." The girl then focuses so intensely on Hermann that the Countess suspects she is in a stupor (333).

Herman and the Countess are brought together with what ultimately seems an uncanny persistence. In fact, they are attracted to each other in what could be termed symmetrical episodes. Without intending to go to the Countess' house, Hermann is mysteriously drawn there twice and looks in her windows. Later, her "ghost" is compelled to come to him, and she looks in his window twice: at the beginning and at the end of her visit. The second time that Hermann is drawn to the Countess' house, an "unknown force" seems to be leading him there. Her "ghost" declares to Hermann that she has come to him "against my will" (349). When they visit each other, both slip unnoticed past sleeping servants. Hermann's spying on the Countess as she prepares for bed and sits in a chair is paralleled as her "ghost" looks in at his window when he awakens and sits on his bed. After causing the Countess' death, Hermann returns to her body twice: while following Lizaveta's directions to leave and by going to the funeral. When he is superstitiously drawn to her funeral, the priest's allusion to death as a "midnight bridegroom" recalls Hermann's thoughts of becoming the Countess' lover when he was first mysteriously drawn to her house. After the Countess' death, her "ghost" apparently returns to screw up her eyes at Hermann twice: by acting through her dead body and via the queen of spades. In these two instances, Pushkin uses similar words to reinforce the apparent haunting: "At that minute it seemed to him that the dead woman mockingly looked at him, screwing up one eye." (348) "At that minute it seemed to him that the queen of spades screwed up her eyes and smiled." (355) In Pushkin's Russian, the two "eye" descriptions are *prishchurivaya odnim glazom* and *prishchurilas'*, respectively; the five translations I have consulted heavily favor "winking."[3]

Various other descriptions tend to associate Hermann with the Countess. When she returns from the ball, we learn that Hermann, hiding in her study, "turned to stone" (*okamenel*). After her death, he passes by her body, which has "turned to stone" (*okamenev*). At the funeral, Hermann, approaching her body, is said to be "pale as the deceased herself." As her corpse seems to screw up one eye, he falls "backwards" (*navznich'*). When she died, the Countess had rolled "over backwards" (*navznich'*) in her chair. This echo connects his apparently causing her death with the first dramatic instance of her potential haunting.

Images of fire provide another link. The Countess wears a hat with ribbons of a "fiery" color (324), and her husband "feared her like fire" (321). Hermann makes "flaming" demands of Lizaveta (345) and has a "fiery" imagination (331). The story about the Countess repeatedly acts upon his imagination (331, 332), and both times Hermann discovers that he has walked to her house without intending to do so.

Just before the Countess dies, Hermann abruptly shifts to the familiar form of address,[4] and her "ghost" addresses him in this same manner. When she dies, the Countess sits in a tall, rectangular-backed armchair which presumably frames her. He then sees her in a rectangular coffin, and her "ghost" is twice framed by his window. All this anticipates Hermann's association of the Countess with the playing-card queen at the end, as Nathan Rosen has shown.[5]

When Hermann spies upon the Countess from her study, she sits in her chair, "swaying to the right and to the left." This swaying, Pushkin adds, seemed to occur "not from her own will, but by the action of a hidden galvanism." (339) As Carl Proffer has suggested, the Countess' involuntary swaying can be related to Hermann's two fateful choices in the story.[6] Lizaveta informs Hermann that he will find two doors in the Countess' bedroom. The right door, she explains, goes to the Countess' study; the left one goes to a winding staircase that leads "to my room." When Hermann arrives:

> On the right was the door leading to the study; on the left, the other one—to the corridor. Hermann opened it, saw the narrow, winding staircase that led to the room of the poor ward . . . But he returned and entered the dark study. (338)

Not only does Hermann actually open the door on the left; as his eyes then focus upon the winding staircase and his thoughts upon its destination, Pushkin's use of the three dots completes our brief but vivid impression that Hermann has chosen to go to Lizaveta's room. Later, at the climax of the story, we read:

> On the right lay the lady, on the left the ace.
> "The ace has won!" said Hermann and turned over his card.
> "Your lady is beaten," Chekalinsky affectionately said.
> Hermann shuddered: instead of the ace, the queen of spades was indeed before him. He did not believe his eyes, was unable to understand how he could have pulled the wrong card. (355)

As before, Pushkin creates the brief illusion that Hermann has chosen "the left" (this time, the ace), whereas he has actually chosen "the right" (the queen). Both choices have disastrous consequences. The first leads to the Countess' loss of life and his loss of a chance to learn her secret; the second, to the loss of his capital and his sanity.

The climactic gambling episode cannot be fully and accurately rendered in English. That the Countess' "ghost" has influenced Hermann's blunder is suggested by his recognizing her corpse's expression on the face of the queen of spades—and by the fact that Chekalinsky's "Your lady is beaten" is, literally, "Your lady is killed" in Pushkin's Russian. The word *laskovo* (literally, "affectionately" or "tenderly'")—applied to Chekalinsky's saying "Your lady is killed"—also resists translation into English. It has been rendered "kindly," "gently," "sweetly," "urbanely," and "genially" in English translations.[7] In the Russian, this word echoes both the initial description of Chekalinsky (352) and the exaggerated politeness with which he greets Hermann the second evening (354). Moreover, the proximity of "affectionately" to "killed" enhances the sinister softness of the web that Fate seems to have been spinning about Hermann and his greedy fixation.

Chekalinsky's role in the story is potentially quite complex. Having acquired the Countess' secret, Hermann thinks of traveling to Paris but, we are told, "An incident saved him the bother." (351) The "incident" is that Chekalinsky happens to have traveled to Petersburg—and also that Narumov happens to bring Hermann to Chekalinsky. When Hermann places his first bet, Chekalinsky is described as "screwing up his eyes" (*prishchurivayas'*). This is one of three uses of the expression in Pushkin's story; as we have seen, the other two describe the Countess' corpse and the queen of spades at the moment of Chekalinsky's victory.

Chekalinsky is said to be a man "of about sixty." This could remind us that the Countess had been repeatedly associated with the phrase "sixty years ago." First, we learn that she was a fashionable flirt in Paris "about sixty years ago" (320); next, she is said to dress just as painstakingly "as sixty years ago" (324). Finally, as Hermann leaves by a secret staircase after the Countess' death, he vividly imagines a young lover she may have had "about sixty years ago" who may have used the same staircase (346). At the funeral, where the priest refers to death as the Countess' "midnight bridegroom," a close relative informs an Englishman that Hermann is the Countess' "natural son." Is it possible, as with the unwitting accuracy of Tomsky's "jokes" to Lizaveta,[8] that this apparent joke is teasingly close to the truth? Is it possible that Chekalinsky, who "screws up his eyes" with Hermann as do the corpse and the queen, who makes possible the Countess' revenge in what resembles a "duel" (355), and who remains almost suspiciously submissive, ingratiating, and even "affectionate" throughout his dealings with Hermann—is actually the Countess' "natural son," conceived about "sixty years" before in a lovers' tryst imagined by Hermann himself, a son, moreover, hypothesized by Hermann just before causing the

Countess' death as he tries to call upon the love she may once have felt for "a newborn son" (340), a son subsequently influenced by the Countess' "ghost" to come to Petersburg in a convenient "incident" so that the Countess' revenge, via the queen of spades, could be complete? This interpretation is particularly tempting because the theme of mistaken identity is so pervasive in Pushkin's works.[9] Here, Hermann is mistaken for Narumov and for Lizaveta's aspiring lover as well. And of course a queen is mistaken for an ace. Is Chekalinsky actually the Countess' sixty-year-old son, who has come to Petersburg to complete by proxy her fateful relationship with Hermann?

The fact that such a possibility can be derived and yet discarded testifies to Pushkin's characteristic detachment from his multi-faceted art. Even in deciding that Chekalinsky, surely, cannot be the Countess' son, we may remember that the story *is* strangely cyclical in nature. Why, for example, are we told at the end that Lizaveta herself has acquired a poor relative as a ward? And why did the Countess' "ghost" declare that she would forgive Hermann her death on the condition that he marry her ward Lizaveta?

The ordering of Pushkin's fictional world in "The Queen of Spades," we may suspect, is based on sequential fateful relationships. The possessors of the gambling secret (after St. Germain) all suffer unenviable fates. The Countess is evidently frightened to death; Chaplitsky, who also wins back his losses, nevertheless dies in poverty; Hermann loses his cherished capital and becomes insane.

All this can be traced to the story's first epigraph: "The queen of spades signifies secret malevolence." The adjective "secret" (*tainuyu*) appears as a noun (*taina*) throughout the story proper: first, with reference to St. Germain's gambling "secret," several times after the Countess acquires it, and once again when it finally becomes Hermann's. It also twice suggests Lizaveta's relationship with Hermann, which, of course, is *his* means of seeking to obtain the gambling secret.

Even the story's present chronology seems fatefully ordered. In Part Two Hermann thinks, of the Countess: "She could die in a week, in two days!" (331) This speculation closely echoes the actual, and patterned, time sequence. Lizaveta first saw Hermann two days after Narumov's evening and a week before Tomsky's visit to the Countess (329). Two days after Lizaveta first sees Hermann, he gives her a letter, and: "In a week, she smiled at him." (330) If the passing of two days is seen as an advancement to the "third day" in a temporal sequence, then these three separate combinations of "two days" and "a week" may all be related to the fateful numbers 1, 3, and 7. (According to the gambling secret, the magic cards are a three, seven, and ace.) When Hermann speculates that the Countess could die in a week or two days, he goes on to decide that his "three sure cards" are calculation, moderation, and industriousness. It is they, he concludes, that "will increase my capital threefold, sevenfold." Rosen summarizes the ingenious attempts of critics to locate an "ace" in this passage, and concludes that it is not there.[10] But as he explains, Nabokov and Tomashevsky have shown that the notion of increasing a unit of money threefold and sevenfold results from letting one's winnings ride twice in a series of three winning wagers. (The wagered amount of money is doubled each time, producing net gains of 1, 3, and 7 original units.) The "ace," or 1, may thus be suggested, quite simply, by the word "capital"—the original unit in Hermann's threefold and sevenfold aspirations. Rosen connects the time at which the "ghost" appears to Hermann with this same numerical sequence. The phrase "a quarter to three" is, in the Russian, 3–1/4 (*bez chetverti tri*), which, Rosen rather ingeniously suggests, "contains the magic numbers 3, 7, 1."[11] He also demonstrates that Hermann had caused the Countess' death at about this same time. And if, as Rosen proposes, the number 3 is missing at the end, when Hermann is incarcerated in room 17, because he had identified a three (of hearts) with Lizaveta's love,[12] the combination 1, 3, 7 is suggested seven times in the story in addition to its three explicit appearances (in Hermann's vision of the "ghost," in his gambling, and in his final insanity).

As we have seen, Hermann was drawn to the Countess by an "unknown force," and after her death, she came to him "against" her "will." The story contains several other references to mysterious or sinister forces. Narumov refers to the Countess' "cabalistics" (323), and Hermann is said to possess "the soul of Mephistopheles" (343). He uses the word "demonic" just before she dies (340), and her bedroom is associated with "Mesmer's magnetism" (338) just before her swaying is related to "a hidden galvanism." Despite its brevity, moreover, the tale contains almost fifty references to death, corpses, the funeral, the deceased, etc. It is thus not entirely surprising that the epigraph to Part Five matter-of-factly describes the nocturnal appearance of a "deceased" baroness, "entirely in white." This anticipates the "white satin dress" worn by the Countess in her coffin (347) as well as the nocturnal appearance of her "ghost" to Hermann "in a white dress" (349) to give him the gambling secret, which, as he attempts to make use of it, completes their fateful relationship—unless, of course, we envision a subsequent encounter.

Notes

1. M. O. Gershenzon saw the tale as essentially realistic, objecting to Belinsky's opinion that it is a fantastic anecdote (M. Gershenzon, *Mudrost' Pushkina*, Ann Arbor, 1983, pp. 97–8, 101–2). More recently, Nathan Rosen has found a supernatural element to be "undeniable," and Carl Proffer has argued that the "ghost's" appearance is part of a dream (Nathan Rosen, "The Magic Cards in *The Queen of Spades*," *Slavic and East European Journal*, Vol. 19, No. 3, fall 1975, p. 258; Carl R. Proffer, *From Karamzin to Bunin*, Bloomington, 1969, pp. 9–10). I have tried to allow for both possibilities.

2. As we can later infer, she may have promised St. Germain never to gamble again— as Chaplitsky did when he reportedly revealed the secret to him—but in her case there is no mention of such a stipulation.

3. Gillon R. Aitken (*The Complete Tales of Alexander Sergeyevich Pushkin*, New York, 1966) has "winked" (300) and "winked" (305).

Rosemary Edmonds (*The Queen of Spades and Other Stories*, New York, 1978) has "winked her eye" (177) and "opened and closed her eye" (182).

T. Keane (*The Poems, Prose and Plays of Alexander Pushkin*, New York, 1936) has "winked with one eye" (583) and "screwed up her eyes" (589).

Ivy and Tatiana Litvinov (*The Queen of Spades and Other Tales*, New York, 1961) have "winked" (39) and "was narrowing her eyes" (44).

Carl R. Proffer (*From Karamzin to Bunin*, Bloomington, 1969) has "winking one eye" (98) and "winked" (103).

4. Hermann's shift reveals a contemptuous anger born of the painful humiliation behind his desperate pleading; the effect is untranslatable into English.

5. Rosen, pp. 267–8.

6. Proffer, p. 9. Harry B. Weber, who proposes that the story is "a new treatment of the Masonic legend of the murder of Hyram-Abif," has likened the Countess' swaying motion to "the moving skeletons in the Masonic anterooms." (*"Pikovaja dama*: A Case for Freemasonry in Russian Literature," *The Slavic and East European Journal*, Vol. 12, No. 4, winter 1968, pp. 435, 440.)

7. Aitken (p. 305), Edmonds (p. 182), Keane (p. 588), the Litvinovs (p. 44), and Proffer (p. 102), respectively.

8. He speculates that "Hermann himself" may have designs on Lizaveta; he also proposes that her admirer may have seen the girl in her own room (343).

9. One thinks of "Mistress into Maid," Burmin (and his wife) in "The Snowstorm," Pugachyov and the Empress in *The Captain's Daughter* (also the hero as traitor and Masha as the priest's niece); in "Angelo," Duk as a monk, Maryana as Isabela, and the head of an outlaw as Clavdio's; Dubrovski as a French tutor, the false Dmitri and Grishka Otrepiev

in *Boris Godunov,* Don Juan as Don Diego in *The Stone Guest,* and the cook in "The House at Kolomna."

10. Rosen, p. 255.

11. *Ibid.,* p. 258.

12. *Ibid.,* p. 270.

Index